Origins of Liberal Dominance

Interests, Identities, and Institutions in Comparative Politics

Series Editor:
Mark I. Lichbach, University of California, Riverside

Editorial Advisory Board:
Barbara Geddes, University of California, Los Angeles
James C. Scott, Yale University
Sven Steinmo, University of Colorado
Kathleen Thelen, Northwestern University
Alan Zuckerman, Brown University

The post-Cold War world faces a series of defining global challenges: virulent forms of conflict, the resurgence of the market as the basis for economic organization, and the construction of democratic institutions.

The books in this series take advantage of the rich development of different approaches to comparative politics in order to offer new perspectives on these problems. The books explore the emerging theoretical and methodological synergisms and controversies about social conflict, political economy, and institutional development.

Democracy without Associations: Transformation of the Party System and Social Cleavages in India, by Pradeep K. Chhibber

Gendering Politics: Women in Israel, by Hanna Herzog

Origins of Liberal Dominance: State, Church, and Party in Nineteenth-Century Europe, by Andrew C. Gould

Origins of Liberal Dominance
State, Church, and Party in Nineteenth-Century Europe

Andrew C. Gould

Ann Arbor
THE UNIVERSITY OF MICHIGAN PRESS

Copyright © by the University of Michigan 1999
All rights reserved
Published in the United States of America by
The University of Michigan Press
Manufactured in the United States of America
♾ Printed on acid-free paper

2002   2001   2000   1999   4   3   2   1

No part of this publication may be reproduced, stored in a retrieval system, or transmitted in any form or by any means, electronic, mechanical, or otherwise, without the written permission of the publisher.

A CIP catalog record for this book is available from the British Library.

Library of Congress Cataloging-in-Publication Data

Gould, Andrew, 1962–
   Origins of liberal dominance : state, church, and party in nineteenth-century Europe / Andrew C. Gould.
     p. cm. — (Interests, identities, and institutions in comparative politics)
   Includes bibliographical references and index.
   ISBN 0-472-11015-2 (cloth : alk. paper)
   1. Europe, Western—Politics and government—19th century. 2. Liberalism—Europe, Western—History—19th century. 3. Church and state—Europe, Western—History—19th century. 4. Political parties—Europe, Western—History—19th century. I. Title. II. Series.
JN94.A58G68   1999
320.94′09′034—dc21   99-33446
                                                                                 CIP

To My Parents

Contents

List of Tables	ix
Acknowledgments	xi
Chapter 1. Origins of Liberalism: Concepts and Explanations	1
Chapter 2. Successful Reform and Conditional Defeat in Belgium	25
Chapter 3. Failed Reform and Contested Victory in France	45
Chapter 4. Failed Reform and Co-opted Defeat in Germany	65
Chapter 5. Successful Reform and Supremacy in Switzerland	87
Chapter 6. Religious Institutions, Reform Dynamics, and Liberalism	115
Bibliography	133
Index	151

Tables

1. Selected Influences on Parties and Regimes in Europe, 1815–1914 — 17
2. Institutions, Reform Dynamics, and Outcomes in Four Countries Compared — 20
3. Institutions, Reform Dynamics, and Outcomes in Belgium — 27
4. Institutions, Reform Dynamics, and Outcomes in France — 47
5. Institutions, Reform Dynamics, and Outcomes in Germany — 67
6. Institutions, Reform Dynamics, and Outcomes in Switzerland — 89

Acknowledgments

My deepest gratitude goes to the many people and institutions whose support aided me in writing this book.

Comparative and historical political science requires the help of librarians. In this case, the librarians who made this research possible were at the University of California at Berkeley, the Archives Générales du Royaume de Belgique, the Bibliothèque Nationale de Belgique, the Paul Hymans Center of the Belgian Liberal Party, the Bibliothèque Nationale in Paris, the Helen Kellogg Institute for International Studies, and the University of Notre Dame.

The Graduate Division of the University of California at Berkeley provided support during early stages of this research. The generous support of the Belgian American Educational Foundation—unfortunately one of Herbert Hoover's least well known legacies—made possible my research abroad. The Graduate Division, the Institute for Scholarship in the Liberal Arts, and the Helen Kellogg Institute for International Studies at the University of Notre Dame all provided support at critical points during the writing of this book.

Three of my teachers at Harvard College inspired me to continue in scholarship: Peter Hall, Terry Karl, and Simon Schama. The comments of graduate school colleagues have been essential to my work, especially in the beginning; my thanks to John Gershman, Michael Gorges, Ollie Johnson, Soo Jin Kim, Robin Silver, Arun Swamy, David Waldner, David Woodruff, and Deborah Yashar. The members of the dissertation committee from which this book is derived helped in distinctive ways: Gerald Feldman provided an historian's perspective and many useful suggestions for sources; Harold L. Wilensky and Andrew C. Janos guided my intellectual development. Giuseppe Di Palma generously took on the task of directing the project after Gregory Luebbert's untimely death.

Many people read and commented upon substantial portions of this project and thereby helped me to improve it. Those not already mentioned are: Chris Ansell, David Blackbourn, Mark Chaves, David Collier, Ruth Collier, Michael Coppedge, Russel Faeges, Robert Fishman, Frederick Fransen, Carol Gould, Jonathan Gould, Tom Kselman, Jonah Levy, Scott Mainwaring, A. James

McAdams, Joel Migdal, Gerry Munck, Guillermo O'Donnell, Ben Ross Schneider, Timothy Scully, Richard Snyder, Lyn Spillman, Jonathan Steinberg, Kathy Thelen, Samuel Valenzuela, Daniel Verdier, and the late Marx Wartofsky. I would also like to thank graduate students at the University of Notre Dame who undertook the delicate task of offering comments to their grader.

For opportunities to present portions of this project I am grateful to the Minda de Gunzberg Center for European Studies at Harvard University, The Helen Kellogg Institute for International Studies at the University of Notre Dame, and the Columbia University Seminar on the Political Economy of War and Peace.

I also wish to thank those who helped in the preparation of the final manuscript, especially to Chuck Myers, Kevin Rennells, and the press's anonymous readers.

In view of all these acknowledgments, any remaining errors in the work must be my own.

Finally, I want to thank my wife, Gretchen Helmke, who has helped me in countless ways. She is my ideal confidante, sounding board, critic, and partner. I am very fortunate to have her as both a personal companion and a professional colleague; with her I learned more than I could have imagined.

This book is dedicated to my parents—Richard and Nancy Gould—for loving learning and for making everything possible.

Chapter 1

Origins of Liberalism: Concepts and Explanations

One of the most fundamental political transitions in Europe in the nineteenth and early twentieth centuries is the emergence of liberalism as a movement for political reform. Liberalism decisively influenced the change from absolutist regimes to constitutional forms of government. Under pressure from liberal reformers, the practices of aristocratic and monarchical rule yielded to new forms of representation with legal protection for private property and distinctions between religious and political authority. Liberal movements did not build these new institutions equally across the region. During the past two hundred years many political conflicts in Europe developed from the widely differing levels of success that liberals attained. The success of liberal movements between 1815 and 1914 ranged from nearly complete supremacy in Switzerland to contested victory in France to conditional defeat in Belgium and to comprehensive defeat and cooptation in Germany.

The goal of this book is to seek explanations for the varied strengths of liberalism in these four countries. Distinct institutional patterns of church-state relations set liberal movements on different developmental paths. Once liberals won initial backing from secular urban elites, the growth of liberal movements rested on gaining support from clergy in various churches and sects. Clergy commanded institutional authority, controlled important organizational resources, and could sway otherwise undecided potential supporters or opponents. In countries where state structures and religious institutions freed clergy from dependence upon the state, then clergy acted independently of authoritarian governments and pursued their own institutional interests. Those clergy who pursued their institutional interests independently often supported liberal reform of the state. While it is not surprising that the clergy who stood to gain in authority through liberal reform of the state favored such reform, the prominent instances of clerical opposition to liberal reform have contributed to the misleading myth of uniformly antiliberal clerical involvement in politics. The truly varied set of clerical responses to the possibility of liberal reform and the relative neglect of this factor (in many theories of development) create the need for a systematic exploration of how religious institutions and leaders shaped the fortunes of liberal parties and the successes or failures that liberals experienced in reforming political regimes.

The possibility of liberal reform provoked different reactions from social groups outside the main urban centers. In no country were secular urban elites or clerical leaders sufficiently strong to give liberals long-term control over national governments. Even adding urban middle and working classes—who offered variable and sometimes crucial support to movements for political reform—does not exhaust the list of social groups important for the success or failure of liberal movements. Liberals faced key obstacles as well as opportunities when they sought support from social groups that later acquired decisive voices under many political systems: provincial middle classes and peasants. Whatever the support for liberal reform among secular and religious elites, the expansion of political participation that occurred throughout Europe in the middle and late nineteenth century made rural support essential for the success of renewed efforts at liberal reform and gave new political significance to the interaction of liberal leaders, clergy, provincial middle classes, and peasants.

Toward a Definition of Liberalism

Nearly every instance of liberalism has produced a different definition of the term. Like many political ideas worthy of sustained inquiry, liberalism has always been complex and varied according to time and place. From the seventeenth century onward, theorists important for liberal thought came from across the European continent: among the most prominent were Adam Smith, John Locke, and John Stuart Mill in the United Kingdom, Benjamin Constant and Germaine de Staël in France, and Immanuel Kant in Germany. Liberal ideas found practical expression in such early documents as the English Bill of Rights of 1689, the American Constitution of 1787, and the Declaration of Rights in the French Constitution of 1789. The term *liberal* first described a political movement around 1812, when it was applied to Spanish Constitutionalists who opposed a renewed absolutist monarchy and was then extended by analogy to movements in Britain and elsewhere (Sauvigny 1970, 150–52). Since 1812, philosophical inquiry and partisan debate in many national contexts reshaped the meaning of the term; it is just one irony of liberalism's history that the meaning of the label in political discourse after World War II in the United States narrowed to "tax-and-spend big government" while it simultaneously came to mean extreme free-market individualism in Europe.

For the purposes of this book, it is essential to recall that liberalism in the nineteenth century had broad connotations emanating from three core elements: constitutional and parliamentary government, economic individualism, and the distinction between religious and political authority. The constitutional and parliamentary aspirations of liberals, the first core element of liberalism, reflected the liberal opposition to the authority of kings and especially the manner in which kings ruled. Liberals sought to replace the unpredictable, arbitrary actions of royal officials with predictable decision making based on written law. From the liberal perspective, the source of sovereignty was the nation, while the legislature (or a monarch and legislature together) made laws that bound the actions of officials. As part of the constitutional order, liberals typically sought a series of rights establishing individual freedoms: freedom of speech, press, and association; an independent judiciary and public trial by jury; as well as civil equality, which involved abolishing any remaining privileges of the nobility and traditional bonds on peasants. These changes in political authority marked the transition from absolutism to constitutional authority.

The second core element of liberalism involved the desire to create and expand markets. Marketization first involved destructive tasks: Liberals sought to end mercantilist policies, royal monopolies, and other restraints on economic activity. Among the traditional restraints on trade that liberals opposed were guild restrictions, local tariffs, and prohibitions on the sale of land. The well-known doctrine of laissez-faire underscored the liberal opposition to mercantilism and internal barriers to trade. Liberals thus followed Adam Smith by arguing that the pursuit of enlightened self-interest within the market would produce public benefits. Marketization also involved the creation of new institutions, such as when liberals established uniform systems of justice that could enforce contracts. Liberals, in other words, sought to create national markets and to adjudicate the disputes that market relations typically entail. They also promoted economic growth through state support for railroads, canals, and port development. These measures established infrastructure for the benefit of commerce and industry and supported specific localities and particular industries—especially coal, iron, steel, heavy machinery, and shipbuilding.

The third principle of nineteenth-century liberalism held that political authority should not settle religious disputes and that religious authority should not settle political disputes. As heirs of the Enlightenment tradition, liberals believed that social order and the regularities of political life emerged from human interactions rather than from divine will. Liberals further claimed that "society can be 'held together' by secular norms and common interests" (Holmes 1993, 263) without additional support from institutional links between church and state. By seeking to remove religious authority from the political realm in this limited way, liberals deprived rulers of an important source of legitimation that rulers had assiduously cultivated. This loss had its compensation for rulers, since liberals freed territorial rulers from the competing claims to religious authority proffered by the many alternative sources (Protestant churches, dissident Protestant sects, the Roman Catholic Church, sectors of the Catholic hierarchy with strong ties to various territorial rulers, and local systems of belief). While it is true that some liberals were hostile to religious belief itself, most confined their opposition to the merging of political and religious authority; the liberal theological claim was that true faith would grow if states ended their corrupt, decayed, and decadent administration of religious affairs.

The threefold common program did not preclude disagreements among liberals about the extent of reform. Most importantly, liberals frequently disagreed over how to consolidate existing gains and many favored halting at limited reforms. Once elections were in place, for example, cautious liberals favored franchise rights for men only and only for those men who met strict financial criteria, indicated by paying substantial taxes. These liberals also distinguished between active citizens, who would exercise the vote along with other civic rights, and passive citizens, who would exercise other civic rights only without the vote. For example, one of French liberalism's frequent ministerial candidates, Adolphe Thiers, argued in the 1830s and most of the 1840s that limiting the number of people who had the right to participate in elections reduced the risk of undesirable and perhaps uncontrollable change. Cautious liberals also favored constitutions with shared authority between a monarch and a legislature and/or a bicameral legislature with a relatively conservative upper house. Most liberals in the nineteenth century believed that the principle of civic equality did not apply to differences between men and women. Yet, on the other side, some liberals advocated extending the basic liberal principles beyond initial reforms in new ways and in new areas. Arguing against Thiers in the late 1840s, Odilon Barrot led the French parliamentary opposition to seek a broader franchise. On the question of gender, a few liberals—notably Mary Wollstonecraft and John Stuart Mill—sought to apply the principle of civic equality to men and women alike. Other liberals seeking broader reforms proposed to diminish a monarch's remaining influence over elected governments or to reduce the authority of a legislature's upper house when it gave too much voice to wealth and status.

Although we can define liberalism as a set of principles accepted by many actors, it is also true that some actors favored different aspects of the liberal program with unequal intensity or accepted only certain parts of the overall package. Distinguishing among degrees of liberalism along the three basic dimensions outlined helps to define the characterization of various liberal movements and their opponents. To take just one example from the cases to come, Belgian liberals advocated private property and free markets, constitutionalism, civic rights, religious freedom, and the separation of church and state, yet on the last dimension of church and state relations, many Belgian liberals still saw a role for the Catholic Church in education until the 1870s. Similar ambiguities in the other cases can also be clarified by examining separately the political, economic, and religious dimensions of liberalism. Likewise, whereas the label conservative unambiguously applies to leaders and movements who rejected each of the three dimensions of the liberal program, it is also true that some leaders and movements accepted parts of the liberal program and opposed others. To use the same national example, Belgian conservatives generally accepted private property and free markets and professed their acceptance of constitutionalism, yet they defended the institutional authority of the church in state education. Belgian liberals and conservatives generally agreed on the economic and political program of liberalism and even agreed on church-state relations for a time yet it was ultimately the religious dimension of the liberal program that distinguished the two parties.

Outcomes to Be Explained: Parties and Regimes

This book is designed to explain the relative strength of liberal political parties and the various types of political regimes between 1815 and 1914. Considering both party strength and regime type facilitates an investigation of how liberalism emerged among groups of political elites with shared ideas, developed organizations of political mobilization, and ultimately shaped the character of political regimes. While one could choose to emphasize either party strength or regime type, an examination of both helps to provide a more accurate description of the fate of liberal ideas when put into practice, especially when characterizing the more intermediate cases in this study. As we will see, several different combinations of party strength and regime type were possible.

Comparing support for liberals to the support offered to other parties provides a measure of the strength of the liberal party. Examining the electoral strength of liberals, I have used historical sources and the writings of historians that employ two labels for identifying early groupings of liberals: parties and movements. Both labels capture important features of the phenomenon of this study. Contemporary readers need to be aware that liberals and their opponents in the nineteenth century spoke of parties before most political scientists today would apply the term (LaPalombara and Weiner 1964). Used in the sense meant by liberals of the early nineteenth century, the term party referred to a group of politicians, political thinkers, writers, publishers, legislative deputies, high-ranking officials, or other elites from among the active political class who shared a general commitment to common principles. Deputies in the early legislatures of the nineteenth century who espoused liberal ideas formed the core of liberal parties; the name of the establishment where the group of deputies met outside the legislature often served as the shorthand name for such a group.

The term *movement*—which early liberals also used—accurately conveys to the contemporary reader the nonspecialized organization of early liberal groups, and I therefore find this term helpful when emphasizing informal organization is important. During periods of relative openness to political activity, for example, leaders organized movements in explicitly political ways, such as when educational societies offered direct support to liberal candidates in elections. During periods of outright repression, liberals organized within social organizations, such as drinking societies, professional associations, recreational societies, and other ostensibly apolitical groups. The full panoply of organizations that now imperfectly fits under the rubric of party was thought to comprise the liberal movement. A related use of *movement* can be found in scholarship on social movements, where it typically applies to groups of the relatively dispossessed seeking means of redress against better organized opponents (Tilly 1988; Tarrow 1994). Liberal movements began as movements of economic, religious, social, and political elites seeking to influence and occupy the leading positions in the state. Even though liberal movements began as elite movements, only the most successful placed their leaders in the top positions in the state, reshaped political regimes, and garnered broader support.

Given the broad time span of this study and the fundamental political changes that took place during this period, we will track liberal groups from their beginnings, when party and movement were virtually synonymous, to the period when we can also observe more functionally specific modern political parties. A minimal definition of a functionally specific modern political party is a group that presents candidates in elections to public office (Sartori 1976, 64). To the set of groups covered by this minimal definition, scholars add the supplement of groups that would do so but cannot either because they are proscribed or because elections are not being held (Collier and Collier 1991, 787). This modification is an entry point for our study of liberal forces under authoritarian conditions, such as in France during the Empire of Louis Napoleon (1851–70). Liberal parties acquired the characteristics of fully modern political parties—namely a permanent bureaucratic staff, extra-parliamentary organization, continuous existence between legislative sittings and elections, and full party controls over the selection of candidates—only in the later part of the nineteenth century and the early twentieth century. These more modern attributes of a political party developed to varying degrees in each of the liberal parties in this study.

While movements and parties are central to the analysis, a more general question addressed in this book is how political regimes developed? I follow Robert Fishman's formulation that a regime comprises "the formal and informal organization of the center of political power, and of its relations with the broader society. A regime determines who has access to political power, and how those who are in power deal with those who are not" (1990, 428). Liberal regimes in the nineteenth century generally moved toward constitutional and parliamentary government, protections for private property in free markets, and distinctions between religious and political authority.

Liberal regimes took two basic forms depending upon the level of formal popular participation in national politics. When participation in national politics remained limited to a narrow elite, liberal movements sought to replace aristocratic and monarchical institutions with new institutions that rooted sovereignty in the nation, such as elections and legislatures. These new regimes also stipulated constitutional procedures for government. Yet such institutions still excluded most people, as few citizens had the right to vote and even fewer had the right to be considered for office. Moreover, constitutional procedures often left some room for monarchical discretion in cabinet formation. Even regimes that were not fully democratic in the contemporary sense can be distinguished from clear failures to transform preliberal institutions. When liberals failed to install new regimes, urban elites gained no greater representation in national parliaments, nor did they secure parliamentary control over government budgets. Where liberalism failed, monarchs successfully reasserted their claim to be the fount of sovereignty, restricted representation to aristocratic status groups, and overrode regular procedures with arbitrary decision making.

If a liberal regime developed when mass participation in national politics was routine, then the regime either supplanted persistent conservative institutions or transformed the previous liberal regime in a democratic direction. Representation in mass-based systems was broader than before—typically involving the extension of suffrage to most adult men, although suffrage laws in the nineteenth century still commonly excluded women and other broad sectors of the population. Once broad participation became institutionalized in the form of mass elections, restrictions on democratic participation were in tension with other essential elements of liberal regimes. Mass-based liberal systems rooted sovereignty in the nation, provided for representation, established constitutional procedures for governance, and limited the institutional connections between church and state. In these systems monarchs and leaders of nonelected institutions decreasingly exercised independent political authority within the state.

Selecting Cases for Comparison

Any empirical study of political development reflects hard choices regarding the country or countries to cover. There are unavoidable trade-offs between the breadth of discussing many cases and the depth that can be explored in just a few cases; there are also trade-offs involved in choosing representative cases or revealingly exceptional ones. Rules for case selection provide important advice for how to handle these choices, yet the application of general rules depends on the state of knowledge in the given field and the types of case selection that have already been employed to develop existing information. In my view, the literature on liberalism can be improved with a new selection of cases for analysis.

The leading studies of liberalism focus on one or two great powers and most emphasize the Anglo-American experience. British liberalism, arguably the most successful liberal movement of the nineteenth century, benefits from intense analysis (Biagini 1996; Jenkins 1988). The connections between religious conflict and support for liberalism in the United Kingdom (Ellens 1994; Parry 1986) prompt the question of whether similar forces were at work in other countries and if not, why not? Yet Anglo-Saxon scholars typically highlight liberalism in the United Kingdom and its former colonies to the detriment of a full examination of the experience of liberal parties on the Continent. Within comparative works, some authors implicitly compare German liberalism to British liberalism but not to other Continental varieties (Dahrendorf 1979 [1967]) or draw insights from an explicit comparison of the United

Kingdom and Germany (Breuilly 1992). Exceptions to this type of focus in studies of liberalism can be found in scholarship that seeks to place German political development in its full European context, as in the work of Dieter Langewiesche (1988a, 1988b, 1990, 1993) and Jürgen Kocka (1986, 1988). While it is difficult to generalize about rich historical work, these studies emphasize the vibrancy of German middle classes and thus raise the questions of how to understand the apparent defeats of German liberal parties and whether a similar understanding applies to other cases. These questions are also forcefully posed by Anglo-American revisionist approaches to German political and social history (Blackbourn and Eley 1984; Blackbourn and Evans 1991; Eley 1991). Anthony Arblaster (1984) and John Hall (1987) situate important liberal theorists within their political contexts and examine crucial events in the United Kingdom, Germany, France, and the United States. Guido de Ruggiero's classic study leaves out the revealing dynamics of liberalism in smaller countries such as Belgium and Switzerland (1981 [1927]).

In contrast to the existing literature, the selection of countries in this paper offers comparisons that are largely new to the study of liberalism. This book's analysis of a different set of cases is an attempt to shed additional light on the liberals' comprehensive victory in Switzerland, contested victory in France, conditional defeat in Belgium, and co-opted defeat in Germany. Even with this new scope, this paper leaves out countries where liberals were least successful, as in Spain, Portugal, Scandinavia, and other countries east and south of Germany and in Italy. By focusing on cases at the center of the distribution of liberal success and failure, the analysis is arguably less open to the potential for distortion that is introduced by examining only the most and least successful liberal movements. This book is thus an attempt to elucidate the building of liberal institutions in cases where liberalism was guaranteed neither success nor failure and where the only guarantee was simply a possibility of success and a possibility of failure.

Explanations Based on Socioeconomic Development and Class

Virtually all major accounts of the rise and fate of European liberalism turn on socioeconomic variables. In these accounts the strength of liberalism is attributed more or less directly to the strength of new economic forces such as high levels of economic development, early industrialization, and growing middle classes. Such variables do help to explain some broad similarities, for as we shall see economic development contributed to the emergence of liberal movements in all these countries. If not supplemented with other factors, however, the result is a conventional perspective that sees the trajectory of liberalism largely in the context of urban economic development. This point of view is not wrong, but it is too narrow. It is not very useful for explaining cross-national variation among the cases that do not fit. Moreover, it does not assess the other causes of liberal success in the most developed societies and the other causes of liberal failure in the least developed societies. While the literature on liberalism is in general quite strong and has recently been reinvigorated with important revisionist historical work, the socioeconomic determinism that has dominated the literature needs to be supplemented with a new approach.

Many works in political science explore the effects of economic development on the character of national political institutions. In Seymour M. Lipset's classic statement: "Perhaps the most common generalization linking political systems to other aspects of society has been that democracy is related to the state of economic development. The more well-to-do a nation, the greater the chances that it will sustain democracy" (1981 [1959], 31). Larry Diamond surveys a vast literature and concludes that "Lipset was broadly correct both in his assertion of a strong causal relationship between economic development and democracy and in his explanations of *why* development promotes democracy" (1992, 485). Andrew Janos offers a more general claim as the central hypothesis of political economy: "as resources become more abundant, it is easier to resolve social conflicts by peaceful means, civil societies are more likely to thrive, and participation in the exercise of authority is more likely to persevere" (1989, 325).

Economic arguments are refined by attention to the timing and character of industrialization and the role of a given type of industrial development within the larger context of the international division of labor. According to these refinements, early development gave economic actors an interest in free trade; entrepreneurs tended to favor individualistic, market-based responses to economic challenges; independent financing kept leading economic actors relatively free of the banks' and government's influence; and relatively small concentrations of capital and labor in industrial enterprises diminished fears that continued market liberalization would diminish the economic position of workers and middle classes (Kurth 1979, 319–62; De Schweinitz 1964; Gerschenkron 1962). For all of these reasons, no study of nineteenth century political development can ignore the character of industrialization (Kitschelt 1992, 1029). Such powerful and interconnected factors as levels of socioeconomic modernization, patterns of economic development, and standing in the international economy form an essential preface to the examination of liberalism in the chapters that follow.

Yet there is evidence that cannot readily be explained by economic factors. France, the Netherlands, and Denmark had similar socioeconomic structures—that is, small firms in the industrial and service sectors and a predominance of the petty bourgeoisie—yet only France had a fully liberal regime in 1875 (Luebbert 1991, 61). In addition, Belgium, Germany, and the Netherlands were more industrialized than France when measured by the proportion of the work force in industry rather than agriculture (Flora and Alber 1987, 494, 460), yet liberals did not dominate in those countries. Common socioeconomic patterns were not associated with similar levels of liberal success. It is equally important to recognize that differences in the timing and character of industrialization did not fully covary with the outcomes for liberal political parties. Belgium had the earliest industrial development on the Continent. But early industrial development was not sufficient to provide a mass base of support under universal suffrage, as we shall see, and Belgian liberals suffered the consequences. French economic development lagged behind Belgian economic development, yet French liberals managed to draw on a mass base of support. In sum, early industrial development cannot account for these instances of liberalism's successes.

Explanations that rely on low state involvement in financing industrialization do not fit comfortably with the evidence from all the cases in this analysis. Two of the cases in this study have been most commonly seen in this light: Germany had bank and state-led industrialization and authoritarian politics, while Switzerland had more entrepreneurial industrialization and liberal politics. In contrast, France, with a powerful central state and late liberal success, and Belgium, with a weak state and late liberal failure, are less commonly given as examples of the impact of the state's role in industrialization because the covariation is not in the expected direction. Moreover, explanations focusing on the types of enterprises in the economy have problems with the timing of industrial concentration and crucial turning points in liberal development. It was only by the end of the nineteenth century that substantial differences emerged between concentration ratios in German and French industry. Yet, a crucial period for liberal politics was 1848–70, during which time industrial concentration rates in Germany and France were quite similar (Luebbert 1991, 59–62, 97–98). Since the patterns of liberal politics were set well before differences in industrial structures developed, decentralized industrial structures were not the sole causes of liberal successes.

An empirical association between socioeconomic modernization and open political regimes does not necessarily imply that economic development is the causal trigger for regime change. I contend that transitions to liberal regimes among the countries of Europe were also relatively independent of economic development and were influenced by the choices of political movement leaders and other elites in the institutions of states and churches. Similarly, Adam Przeworski and Fernando Limongi argue that transitions to democracy are equally likely at all levels of economic development after 1950; on the basis of partial data for democracies before 1950, they argue that the levels at which democracies emerged were highly scattered (1997, 173).

By emphasizing how appropriate types of industrialization can liberalize political systems, many theories do not pay sufficient attention to the effects of different starting points. Theories that focus on types of industrialization circumscribe the historical and political context in which industrialization takes place. Political systems can be liberalized in a number of different ways; liberal reformers face easy choices in some situations and difficult ones in others. Economic development sufficient to provoke political change in one setting may not be adequate for provoking change in another setting. National differences in industrialization cannot fully explain the different political outcomes; a complete analysis must also refer to the political and religious institutions that provoked and guided political action.

Notwithstanding a debate over the efficacy of economic arguments, one of the most important themes in studies of liberalism is the politics of the middle class. There is much to support a view that the rise of the middle classes caused liberalism to triumph. Anthony Arblaster, for example, identifies the start of political liberalism at the end of the seventeenth century in the Netherlands and England, the two countries where the bourgeoisie were the strongest; in the rest of Europe, by contrast, "feudal absolutism was firmly established" wherever "the landed aristocracy continued to dominate" (1984, 146). In Harold Laski's words,

> In the period between the Reformation and the French Revolution a new social class established its title to a full share in the control of the state. . . . The control of politics by an aristocracy whose authority was built upon the tenure of land came to be shared with men whose influence was derived solely from the ownership of movable capital. . . . New material conditions, in short, gave birth to new social relationships; and, in terms of these, a new philosophy was evolved. . . . This new philosophy was liberalism. (1936, 1–2)

More fine-grained analyses argue that political coalitions were shaped primarily by economic interests of various economic groups. For example, it has been argued that a coalition of "iron and rye" backed antiliberalism in Germany, while a similar coalition of "steel and wheat" pushed a conservative line in France (Wehler 1985; Elwitt 1975; Lebovics 1988). In this view, a social class bears a distinctive political ideology, and the waxing of a class's economic and social power causes its particular ideology to become more influential over other social classes and within a given society as a whole.

According to this perspective, a decline in the middle class's enthusiasm for liberal reform can be attributed to the rise of the working class and its demands for social justice. With the rise of the French working class, according to Karl Marx's famous analysis of the events surrounding the Revolution of 1848, "every demand of the simplest bourgeois financial reform, of the most ordinary liberalism, of the most formal republicanism, of the most insipid democracy, is simultaneously castigated as an 'attempt on society' and stigmatized as 'socialism'" and then cast aside in favor of authoritarianism (1977 [1852], 25). Alexis de Tocqueville, although himself a member of the nobility, was just one of many liberals who showed little sympathy for the politically active working classes in 1848—as his memoirs reveal—and the Parisian uprising in June pushed him to quite conservative positions (Jardin 1988, 416).

The mere emergence of a particular social class should be carefully distinguished from the undeniable influence of what was called "the social question." It was not the presence of misery among increasing numbers of workers that chastened liberals, but the actions of new social and political movements. Guido de Ruggiero carefully put it like this: "The appearance of Socialism on the political stage in the second half of the nineteenth century, and the rapid progress which it made, created a profound perturbation in the Liberal mind" (1981 [1927], 381). Ruggiero's emphasis on the rise of socialism, a political movement, rather than the working classes per se, is in the spirit of my analysis. A careful distinction between a social class and social and political movements is required in a comparative perspective because classes and movements had variable relationships. For example, where liberals succeeded in the period of mass politics, as Aristide Zolberg's study of Western European political development concludes, workers supported more reformist political parties (1986).

In my view, the political actions of people, even those in similar economic situations, reflect political calculations not just raw economic interests. While economic conditions cannot be ignored in a complete study, there are also noneconomic determinants of how actors identify their interests and make choices in the political realm. In a study of liberalism, we cannot assume that the middle classes in one country took the natural political position of a middle class and that other national middle classes took positions more or less removed from the ideal (Blackbourn and Eley 1984; Evans 1987; Rueschemeyer, Stephens, and Stephens 1992, 101, 145). As these scholars argue, we need to focus on the variable political choices of actors without privileging the choice of any one actor as the expected choice for an entire set of similar actors. There is also a more interpretivist, political constructionist parallel to the effort here. Politics—even workplace politics—is shaped by social organizations and ideologies in addition to market and technological forces (Sabel 1982; Tolliday and Zeitlin 1992). Social classes are not just objectively defined, that is, by their position in the division of labor or by their material conditions. Rather, actors define themselves politically and understand their relations with other actors through particular struggles and with the aid of ideas of self-interest. An analyst has to consider a social actor in a particular context, for it is there (and perhaps only there) that the analyst can discover why social actors pursue particular political goals with specific strategies.

In sum, there is a need to supplement socioeconomic and class-based approaches with a comparative-historical approach that places a new emphasis on the structuring role of political institutions. With respect to the socioeconomic approach, I have argued that such approaches cannot fully account for historical variations in the success and failure of liberalism. Similarly, the tendency of class-based approaches to reduce liberalism to a program for the emancipation of the middle class does not fit with the broad variety of groups that supported liberal movements or with the many instances in which middle classes did not support liberalism. By identifying the role of religious institutions and their interaction with political actors, this book builds on both macrohistorical and actor-centered insights developed in comparative-historical analyses of institutions. Drawing on these perspectives, I shall argue, allows us to make sense of the range of outcomes that marked nineteenth-century European liberalism.

Structures and Choices in an Institutional Context

Many scholars working in the tradition of comparative-historical analysis examine the role that political institutions play in shaping diverse outcomes. For example, Gregory Luebbert contends that divergent levels of success in the building of nineteenth-century liberal regimes led to different modes of labor mobilization and alternative types of political regimes in interwar Europe

(1991). The institutional approach is prominent in the literature on political parties, but it is also developed in the field of political economy by historical institutionalists who maintain that institutions organize the interactions of social actors and thereby affect the outcomes of those interactions (Steinmo and Thelen 1992, 3). A common theme among these diverse scholars is the idea that differences in the institutions of state and society, and especially in the institutions that mediate the relationship of state and society, generate various responses to common forces or similar events (Locke and Thelen 1995, 342).

While there are many institutional relations of potential importance, some scholars of European political development have focused in particular on the setting provided by religious and political institutions. Pioneering this approach, Seymour M. Lipset and Stein Rokkan view the impact of religion on political development largely through the interaction of states and churches, especially in the Reformation and during the expansion of public education in the nineteenth century. Their perspective emphasizes that institutional conflicts leave legacies in the form of social cleavages, which, in turn, affect the configuration of party systems (Lipset and Rokkan 1967; Lipset 1968, 169–95; Flora 1983a, 11–26). John Madeley focuses this optic on the Protestant countries of Western Europe and argues that distinctive eighteenth-century church-state regimes, reinforced in their differences by nineteenth-century religious revivals, produced divergent types of Protestant religious parties (1982, 160). John H. Whyte reaches similar conclusions in his study of Catholic political behavior in Western democracies (1981, 126–27). Extending these analytical tools to a non-European case, Timothy Scully argues that the clerical-anticlerical cleavage organized political space in the nineteenth and early twentieth centuries and then defined "intraelite, as well as fundamental party identities, well into the twentieth century" (1992, 63). Following in this tradition, I seek to show that we can understand the development of liberal parties and regimes by focusing on the religious and political institutions out of which liberals emerged and which liberals then sought to transform.

Even though institutional approaches have a distinguished pedigree in political science, the recent flowering of rational choice scholarship encourages institutionalists to clarify their arguments in a number of key areas. In explaining the choices of a given social actor, rational choice scholars emphasize not only the opportunities and constraints presented by institutions, but also the strategies of other important actors and the possibility that new actors may emerge. In seeking solutions to collective action problems more generally, rational choice institutionalists examine the role that institutions such as community and hierarchy play in the decision making of actors and also the possibility that other institutions such as markets and contracts may emerge from actions (Lichbach 1996, 18–24). These insights do not imply that rational choice approaches must replace institutional approaches, rather, as Elinor Ostrom argues, "a real convergence is occurring as more political scientists presume that individuals are rational and search for institutional structures to help explain behavior. . . . [R]ational choice and institutional analysis are likely to be essential complements" (1991, 241–42).

Institutional and rational-choice approaches—when fully developed—modify each other. For example, Stathis Kalyvas argues that the macrohistorical approach to political parties needs to be supplemented with the "microfoundations" essential for understanding how political processes produce mobilization and organization. Kalyvas criticizes overly simple macrohistorical perspectives for asserting that a politicized religious identity caused the formation of confessional parties, when it is equally important to see that the formation of confessional parties caused the politicization of religious identity (1996). Drawing on this lesson, my structural account of the development of liberal parties and regimes does not assert that identities preceded organization; similarly I avoid arguing that structural causes operated at great historical remove from their hypothesized effects or that structures prevented actors from pursuing their rational interests. Instead, I seek to link religious and political institutions to the dynamics of political reform, that is, to the strategies that liberal parties pursued and to the responses offered by various other political actors.

Explaining Liberal Parties and Regimes through Prior
Institutions and Reform Dynamics

This book explores the interplay between institutions and attempts to reform them. Institutions set the frame for change by providing the context in which political struggles took place. More than the context alone, institutions also served as the target for reform attempts, since the institutions of state led the list of those that liberals sought to transform. Finally, institutions shaped the incentives for support or opposition that various groups experienced when deciding what positions to take with respect to possible reforms. Context, target, and incentive structure all derived from institutions prior to the onset of reform. Once reform was underway, and at least partially successful, these elements changed and recombined to alter the possibilities for further reform. The basic steps in this historical argument may be seen in table 1.

TABLE 1. Selected Influences on Parties and Regimes in Europe, 1815–1914

Elite Phase

State and Church Institutions at Onset of Liberal Reform → Liberal Policy toward Religious Authority → Response of Clergy → Fate of Liberal Reform → To Mass Phase

Mass Phase

Institutions at Onset of Second Liberal Reform → Liberal Policy toward Religious Authority → Response of Clergy → Provincial Middle-Class and Peasant Reply → Party and Regime Outcome

My analysis distinguishes two phases of political development to highlight the crucial transition from elite-based systems to mass-based systems. The first set of interactions investigated here took place under the conditions that I describe as elite politics, typically during the first two-thirds of the nineteenth century, when national politics was the domain of status and class elites. Elite-driven politics were normal postrevolutionary politics; most people observed social conventions—such as deference to status elites—even when acting politically. Suffrage systems offering the franchise on an unequal basis—typically according to tax payments, wealth, and office-holding—provided the legal framework for the disproportionate influence of elite groups. Under these conditions, groups at the top of the social order in urban and rural areas were critical to the stability of political regimes, making liberals and clerical elites the key actors. The second set of interactions, typically during the last third of the century, took place as the mass of people in each country exercised routine influence on national political outcomes. Under mass politics, most adult men exercised the right to a secret ballot in reasonably free elections; other expressions of public opinion such as in newspapers and popular organizations also forced government responses; in addition, states increased their direct contact with individual citizens through mass systems of primary education. Under mass conditions, the key actors in political coalitions therefore broadened from liberals and clerical elites to include provincial middle classes and peasants as well.

The analysis begins with the institutions of state and church at the onset of liberal reform. These prior institutions set the frame for liberal reform proposals, since liberals aimed at transforming aspects of regimes that did not match their ideals. Liberals proposed reforms that moved regimes toward constitutional and parliamentary government, private property in free markets, and distinctions between religious and political authority. Where more than one religious organization was present, as in the countries with substantial Catholic and Protestant churches, liberals had to take positions with respect to each religious organization. Various clergy responded to these proposals according to the ways that liberal reform affected their institutional interests compared to the existing regime. To a large degree, we shall see that clerical responses to liberal reform shaped the fate of liberal reform. The outcome of liberal reform in the elite phase involved either the successful establishment of parliamentary sovereignty or its failure and renewed executive sovereignty by a monarch or emperor.

The analysis then turns to the mass phase. Working in the context of newly broadened societal participation and the institutions inherited from the previous phase, liberals attempted a second set of reforms to either preserve their gains or overturn nonconstitutional regimes. These reforms had consequences for churches and clerical authority and clergy responded according to the alternative frameworks for institutional authority open to them. Given the broader context of political participation in the mass phase, liberal strategies and clerical responses involved appeals to provincial middle classes and peasants. These new actors in routine national politics replied with varied levels of support for liberals, clergy, and other political organizers. As we shall see, the alignment of provincial middle classes and peasants exercised a great influence on the fate of the second attempt at liberal reform. The outcomes in this phase involved various levels of mass support for liberal parties and distinct degrees of success or failure in establishing liberal political regimes.

Organization of the Argument

I seek to explain varying outcomes across four countries. This book thus examines changes over time in each case while also placing the cases in comparative perspective. Table 2 permits one to see the basic outlines of each case over the entire period and in comparison with the others. Since the steps in the argument are the same for each case, the elements from the previous figure serve as the row labels in table 2. Each column represents a case and each cell entry describes how that case fits into a given step in the overall argument.

One of the intermediate cases in this analysis is Belgium. Belgian liberals established a liberal regime in the 1830s. In terms of popular support, liberals predominated in elections from 1847 to 1883. Nevertheless, from 1884 on the Catholic party won every election and formed every government. Most of the basic elements of the regime remained unchanged, but legislation in the 1880s returned control over education to the Catholic Church and thereby the newly modified regime strongly favored broad authority for clergy. Thus, the Belgian liberal movement achieved its greatest successes in the elite phase while in the mass phase it survived but suffered some defeats. How can these outcomes in Belgium be explained? Why did liberals succeed in the elite phase? What permitted the subsequent run of liberal predominance? Why did pro-church politicians finally reverse their fortunes and assume leadership in the Belgian regime?

The answers to these questions will be explored more fully in the next chapter, but readers may wish to see the main lines of the analysis of Belgium here. The institutions prior to reform were a neoabsolutist monarchy in which a Protestant monarch was largely opposed to the Catholic Church. Liberals

TABLE 2. Institutions, Reform Dynamics, and Outcomes in Four Countries Compared

	Germany	Belgium	Switzerland	France
Elite Phase				
State and Church Institutions at Onset of Liberal Reform	Non-liberal Incorporated Churches	Non-liberal Church not incorporated	Non-liberal Churches not incorporated	Non-liberal Incorporated Church
Liberal Policy toward Religious Authority	Attack Protestant Attack Catholic	Promote Catholic	Preserve Protestant Attack Catholic	Attack Catholic
Response of Clergy	Opposition Opposition	Support	Support Opposition	Opposition
Fate of Elite Liberal Reform	**Failed**	**Successful**	**Successful**	**Failed**
Mass Phase				
Institutions at Onset of Second Liberal Reform	Monarchs sovereign	Parliament sovereign	Parliament sovereign	Emperor sovereign
Liberal Policy toward Religious Authority	Preserve Protestant Attack Catholic	Attack Catholic	Preserve Protestant Attack Catholic	Attack Catholic
Response of Clergy	Toleration Opposition	Opposition	Support Opposition	Opposition
Provincial Middle-Class and Peasant Reply	Tolerate liberals Oppose liberals	Oppose liberals	Support liberals Oppose liberals	Support liberals
Party and Regime Outcome	**Co-opted Defeat of Liberals** Weak liberal parties in an authoritarian regime	**Conditional Defeat of Liberals** Weak liberal party in a constitutional democracy	**Supremacy of Liberals** Strong liberal parties in a constitutional democracy	**Contested Victory of Liberals** Strong liberal party in a contested constitutional democracy

opposed the monarch and offered to enhance Catholic Church authority by granting it greater freedom to organize in a newly independent state; clergy supported prochurch politicians and their alliance with liberals. This first attempt at liberal reform succeeded in the form of constitutionalism and a sovereign parliament with a largely autonomous Catholic Church. During the mass phase, liberals sought mainly to attack Catholic Church authority. Catholic clergy opposed liberals and aided prochurch politicians seeking to break with the ruling liberals. Catholic provincial middle classes and peasants opposed liberals and accepted mobilization by the Catholic party. Thus, we shall see that the Belgian liberals first enhanced clerical authority and then sought to curtail it, thereby achieving early successes but suffering a conditional defeat as the party became electorally weak within a modified constitutional democracy.

The other intermediate case is France. In the elite phase, formal regime institutions matched many liberal ambitions, yet each of the three attempts to sustain constitutional regimes prior to 1851 led to executives that circumvented liberal procedures and all three regimes fell to a revolution or a coup. As for popular support, liberals rarely had a majority in the elected assemblies from 1815 to 1851. With only partially liberalized regimes and difficulty in building support among elites it is hard to say that French liberals achieved their main aims in the first phase. In the latter third of the century, however, the fortunes of mainstream liberals—Republicans—changed for the better and cooperation with center-right liberals amplified this success. Republicans won support in urban areas in the elections of 1869, secured a majority in the assembly in 1876, and won a broad national mandate in 1877. Republicans anchored a regime-founding coalition of liberals from the center-right to the center-left that passed the key constitutional provisions of what came to be known as the Third Republic. Even with these accomplishments, however, the development of French liberalism continued to be characterized by setbacks, compromises, and periodically renewed challenges from the right. Thus one may summarize the experience of French liberals by noting their difficulties in the elite phase and greater successes in the mass phase.

Why did liberals fail to preserve parliamentary institutions in the elite era? Why did liberals successfully reestablish parliamentary institutions in 1871–79? Why did right-wing forces periodically challenge yet repeatedly fail to topple liberal institutions built on a mass base?

The account below emphasizes key features of the interaction between institutions and the dynamics of reform in France that render this pattern of early setbacks and later victories understandable. The institutions of state and church prior to reform involved a neoabsolutist Catholic monarchy allied to the Catholic Church. Liberals attacked both and sought to curtail the authority of the Catholic Church. In their response, clergy opposed liberals by allying with aristocrats and monarchs. The outcomes in the elite phase thus were stalemated and failed liberal reform in which the executive rather than the legislature emerged as sovereign. In the mass phase, with the executive allied with the Catholic Church, liberals attacked clerical authority. Catholic clergy opposed liberals and again aided aristocrats and potential monarchs. Peasants in southeast and provincial middle classes accepted liberal mobilization to counter the Catholic strategy, thus providing a popular basis for the victory of a strong liberal party in a constitutional democracy. Peasants elsewhere and a minority of the provincial middle classes retained loyalties to antisystem opposition groups, thus rendering the liberal victories contested at several key moments.

Where liberals were least successful, they managed to build only an electorally weak liberal party in a nonliberal political regime as in German states for most of the nineteenth century. On the dimension of support for the party, German liberals occasionally achieved the levels of popular support enjoyed by liberals in the other cases in this analysis, such as in the spring of 1848 when elections to the Frankfurt constitutional assembly and to various parliaments in several German states revealed substantial popular support for liberal candidates and from 1858 to 1863 when liberals occupied about two-thirds of the seats in the Prussian parliament. Yet for the rest of the nineteenth century the indicators of liberal electoral strength are much weaker. From 1867 through 1876 liberals occupied about half the seats in the German parliament; from 1877 to 1890 liberals typically won just over a third of all votes in elections to the parliament; and in every subsequent election until 1912 liberals won less than 29 percent of the vote. On the dimension of regime, in neither the elite nor the mass phases of politics did German liberals succeed in dislodging authoritarian practices. While a few of the German states adopted liberal constitutions in the 1830s, the liberals' attempt to unify German states under a liberal regime in 1848 foundered. Several post-1848 reforms brought elements of liberal constitutionalism into the formal structure of states, but executives successfully resisted attempts to turn laws into actual practice with respect to legislative sovereignty and control of government budgets, notably in Prussia in the early 1860s. The unification of many German states under Prussian auspices in 1870 imposed an illiberal, if formally constitutional, regime that was not fundamentally reformed before its overthrow in 1919.

Why were the victories of German liberals strong in economic and social realms but weak in the political realm? Why were predominantly Protestant liberals unsuccessful in attracting support from Protestant clergy? Why was cooperation between Protestant liberals and Catholic politicians—two groups at odds with state executives—so limited?

As we shall see more fully below, the prior institutions in the German states were neoabsolutist monarchies with established Protestant churches and an allied Catholic Church. In their opposition, liberals took a similar position with respect to religious authority in Protestant and Catholic churches: liberals attacked and sought to curtail both churches' authority. Most clergy of both confessions allied with monarchs. The first efforts at liberal reform failed, as none of the major states adopted effective constitutions and monarchs retained their sovereignty. In the second round of reform, liberals sought to retain the authority of Protestant churches but attacked the authority of the Catholic Church. Protestant clergy in Prussia aided conservatives and tolerated the strategic alliance of conservatives with liberals. Catholic clergy aided pro-church politicians in opposition to both Protestant conservatives and liberals. The reply of Protestant provincial middle classes and peasants involved toleration for liberals in Prussia and support for liberals elsewhere; Catholics in the same classes accepted mobilization by a Catholic party. Thus, the outcome for the German case involved a co-opted defeat of liberals that was characterized by weak liberal parties in an overall authoritarian regime.

Where liberals succeeded most fully, they founded liberal political parties that won strong electoral support and built liberal political regimes. This outcome may be seen in this study in the Swiss case. At the level of electoral support, Swiss liberals exercised near hegemony in their political system in both the elite and mass phases. Switzerland's mainstream liberal party—the Radicals—won more votes than any other party in every legislative election from 1848 to 1917. They controlled an outright majority of the seats in the national legislature after 17 of the 23 elections between 1848 and 1914. At the level of the regime, Swiss liberals succeeded in both elite and mass periods by founding constitutional regimes in the 1830s in most localities and by extending these gains to the national level in 1847. In the 1870s, new protections for the right to vote and new institutions of referendum and initiative transformed liberal constitutionalism in a democratic direction without altering other basic liberal principles.

Few scholars subject the Swiss experience to probing questions of political development, for its relatively early economic development and the near absence of a feudal landed elite or extensive military bureaucracy seemed to render liberal political outcomes less problematic. Notwithstanding the importance of these characteristics, however, important questions remain. Why did liberals seek to transform anything about Swiss political regimes? Why were Protestant clergy relatively neutral in these struggles compared to Catholic clergy? Why did religion—and not language or region—serve as the principle cleavage in Swiss political development and how did it affect the fortunes of Swiss liberalism?

Although Switzerland lacked a monarch, the prereform urban oligarchies ruled cities and their surrounding countryside in ways that were far from egalitarian or constitutional. In addition, each local oligarchy had an established Protestant church or an allied Catholic Church. Liberal reformers sought to retain Protestant clerical authority but curtail Catholic clerical authority. Protestant clergy supported liberals while Catholic clergy opposed them and even sought support from foreign monarchs. Thus the outcome of the elite phase of reform involved especially strong liberal forces in Protestant areas and a strongly liberal national constitution. The Protestant churches remained established on a local basis only, while the Catholic Church sought to expand its activities in a hostile environment. In the mass phase, liberals again sought to preserve Protestant churches and curtail Catholic Church authority. Protestant clergy supported liberals while Catholic clergy aided prochurch politicians. Among the provincial middle classes and peasants, Protestants supported liberal parties while Catholics opposed liberals and accepted mobilization by a Catholic party. The resulting supremacy of strong liberal parties in a constitutional democracy preserved liberal gains for many years, even to the exclusion of contemporary forms of social liberalism and gender equality for much of the twentieth century.

While the chapters can be read in any order, they appear here so as to investigate the intermediate outcomes regarding liberal success and failure first. Thus, chapter 2 considers the early successes and mitigated defeat of Belgian liberals and chapter 3 explores the contested achievements of French liberalism. The book then turns to the two cases where liberals achieved more consistent results: chapter 4 studies the repeated difficulties liberals encountered in Germany and chapter 5 examines the more positive fortunes of liberals in Switzerland. Chapter 6 reflects on an additional paradigmatic case and examines how distinct institutions of religious and political authority and their interaction with rural social groups contributed to the success of British liberalism. The chapter concludes with implications of this study for our understanding of transitions to democracy, the consolidation of liberal regimes, and the relationship of liberalism and democracy.

Chapter 2

Successful Reform and Conditional Defeat in Belgium

The experience of Belgian liberalism challenges the commonly held view that advanced economic development and a middle-class society fully account for the success of liberalism. Belgium had the conditions thought to be favorable to the creation and maintenance of liberal institutions: early industrial development, rising overall welfare, politically active middle classes, free agricultural labor, and few landed elites defending the privileges of aristocratic status. Yet, despite these favorable circumstances, the development of Belgian liberalism followed a pattern that suggests possibilities for further analysis. Each of the three stages—precocious liberal success from 1815 to 1846, dominance in government from 1847 to 1884, and marginalization from 1884 to 1914—can be accounted for only by exploring the interaction of the Catholic Church and liberal anticlericalism. Given that economic and social-structural accounts have already helped us to understand many important aspects of nineteenth century liberalism, it is now time to incorporate other insights, especially those that can be developed by focusing on the consequences of religious institutions.

A country's political institutions demand a more complete explanation, especially when those institutions strongly influence theory building. The early liberal reform, the struggles between liberals and Catholics, and the subsequent Catholic party dominance set the stage for the emergence of what Arend Lijphart terms a consociational or consensus democracy (Lijphart 1977, 1984). Under constitutional innovations in the 1970s, Belgium adopted limits on majoritarian rule that made it "a complete example of consociational democracy: it is the most perfect, most convincing, and most impressive example of a consociation" (Lijphart 1981, 8). Lijphart interprets the reforms of the 1970s as a "formal continuation of informal consociational practices [such as the Unionist governments of the 1830s and 1840s] that have long been used for the solution of religious and ideological conflicts" (1981, 11). A full examination of the political impact of linguistic (Flemish/French/bilingual) and cultural (Fleming/Walloon/Bruxellois) cleavages lie outside the scope of this chapter, but it is important to note that the cooperation and conflict between liberals and Catholics created institutions that both provoked and channeled conflict over language and culture in distinctive ways (Lorwin 1966, 1971; Zolberg 1978; Huyse 1981).

This chapter's argument is that religious institutions and the dynamics of reform decisively shaped Belgium's political outcomes. First, the crucial push for the creation of liberal institutions came from anticlerical liberals and prochurch political Catholics working together because of their shared interests in national independence and their support for a constitutional regime. Next—when international recognition of Belgian sovereignty by the 1840s dissolved the shared interests of anticlericals and Catholic Church supporters—liberals broke with the compromise position and won control of the government alone. In the middle years of the nineteenth century, liberal dominance rested on restricting participation to those likely to share anticlerical views—via a narrow franchise and careful manipulation of voter rolls—and the partial compliance of prochurch political leaders. Finally, the policy implementation of liberal anticlericalism broke the remaining consensus at the elite level and the narrow electorate rejected liberals at the polls in the critical election of 1884. Anticlerical policies simultaneously encouraged a revival of popular religiosity and a new form of Catholic mass organization for politics; when the peasantry became fully active in national politics, in the late 1880s and 1890s, liberals suffered a lasting decline in influence.

Consensus across the Religious Divide: 1830–47

In order to begin illustrating how religious institutions contributed decisively to the development of liberalism, I now turn to the early period of Belgian political development. Belgian liberalism in the early nineteenth century was typical of European liberalism, including the social groups to which it appealed, its program, and its definition of potential allies and opponents. Liberals in Belgium, as throughout Europe, gained support from urban upper classes. Belgian liberals controlled virtually every city council after 1830 and dominated the parliamentary delegations elected from urban areas. They earned this support under conditions of elite politics, that is, when only a small part of the population participated in national politics and when the typical forms of political organization included personal networks, elite political clubs, early newspapers, and only rudimentary formal political organizations. The restrictions on the right to vote reflected the narrowness of political participation in Belgium: less than 5 percent of the adult male population until 1847 and less than 10 percent until 1893 had the right to vote in national elections.

TABLE 3. Institutions, Reform Dynamics, and Outcomes in Belgium

Elite Phase

State and Church Institutions at Onset of Liberal Reform	*Non-liberal, church not incorporated* Neo-absolutist, Protestant monarchy in the Netherlands opposed to Catholic Church in southern provinces imposed by 1815 Congress of Vienna
Liberal policy toward Religious Authority	*Promote* Offer Catholic Church autonomy in 1830 Revolution and independent Belgium
Response of Clergy	*Support* Clergy and prochurch politicians support independence and liberal constitution
Fate of Elite Liberal Reform	**Successful** Independence and constitution achieved 1830 and unionist governments to 1846

Mass Phase

Institutions at Onset of Second Liberal Reform	*Parliament sovereign* Catholic Church more autonomous
Liberal Policy toward Religious Authority	*Attack* Curtail Catholic Church authority through education law of 1879
Response of Clergy	*Opposition* Boycott state schools and promote church schools and partisan organizing
Provincial Middle-Class and Peasant Reply	*Oppose liberals* Catholics accept mobilization by prochurch Catholic party
Party and Regime Outcome	**Conditional Defeat of Liberals** *Weak liberal party in a constitutional democracy* Catholic party becomes majority party in 1884 and grants public educational authority to clergy, but otherwise retains liberal constitution

Few liberal movements were as successful at building liberal institutions. The Constitution of 1831 enshrined classical liberal rights, such as freedom of association, the right to a fair trial, and freedom from arbitrary arrest. Moreover, the constitution asserted the sovereignty of parliament over the authority of the king. On the economic dimension, the Belgian state vigorously protected the rights of private property over and against traditional restrictions. The accomplishment of the Belgian liberals should also be seen in its religious context: Belgium was an overwhelmingly Catholic country whose political class, liberals included, were virtually all Catholic, at least nominally. How, in light of the many similarities between Belgian liberals and their counterparts elsewhere on the continent and Belgium's Catholic culture, can the exceptional success of Belgian liberals in building liberal institutions be explained?

An important cause of cross-national variation in the strength of liberalism under elite politics was the nature of the relationship between urban liberals and clergy. Liberals typically dominated the cities, but where urban liberals and clergy could form an alliance, then liberals dominated much of the political system. Such an alliance was the pattern in Belgium; urban liberals and clergy concurred on the importance of seeking independence from the Dutch crown, which had been granted authority over Belgium in the restoration settlement of 1815. Each group, with different ends in view, favored independence from the Netherlands as a means. For their part, urban liberals sought to free themselves from the autocratic powers of the Dutch king, while clergy, for their part, sought religious freedom for the Catholic faith, which was restricted by the Protestant House of Orange. Liberals opposed the nonconstitutional political regime of the Dutch king; Catholics chafed under Protestant rule. Together, liberals and political Catholics opposed the Dutch crown in the Revolution of 1830, gained the independence of Belgium, and authored a constitutional compromise of liberal and Catholic interests.

Liberals and political Catholics cooperated in order to resist a common enemy, the Dutch House of Orange, in the struggle for Belgian independence. Until the issue was settled by international acceptance of Belgian separateness from the Netherlands, the main feature of Belgian politics was the drive for independence from the Dutch crown. From independence in 1830 until 1847 all governments were self-proclaimed "unionist" governments, whose policy toward that end was the permanent compromise between liberal and prochurch positions. The cabinets of unionist governments, for example, included liberals and political Catholics. Governments were nearly always supported by a joint liberal and prochurch majority and were typically opposed by a fluid "party of movement;" political Catholics did not oppose liberals as such (Stengers 1965).

The consensus position extended even to the issue that would later drive liberals and political Catholics apart, the role of the church in education. At least until 1846, the official consensus over the content and function of primary instruction asserted that education ought to include the moral guidance of religious instruction in the interest of social stability (Gubin and Lefèvre 1985, 334).[1] According to this view, priestly control of religious instruction best insured socially necessary moral guidance. The anticlerical/clerical cleavage was thus initially muted by a subtending convergence of interests between urban liberals and rural notables and a mutual understanding among leading politicians.

Belgium's early industrial development did not uniformly work to the advantage of political liberalism. Leading industrialists opposed the Revolution of 1830 and advocated the return to sovereignty over Belgian provinces of the Dutch House of Orange. Industrialists were skeptical about independence from the Netherlands, for it seemed to portend the loss of markets. For the most part, "Orangists" shared with liberals their views on economic policy and an anticlerical attitude toward the Catholic Church (Witte and Craeybeckx 1987, 21, 37). Other industrialists supported unification with France instead for access to its large market. The hopes of Orangists and French nationalists were dealt severe blows by foreign developments. As for the French claim, Louis Philippe renounced any authority over Belgium shortly after the Revolution of 1830. As for the Dutch, the House of Orange acknowledged Belgium's independent sovereignty with the Treaty of Twenty-Four Articles in 1839. Most Orangists left the movement in the years shortly after the Revolution of 1830 to join the liberal movement. As the alternatives to independence became less likely, Orangists moved into the liberal camp, but common interests of liberals and prochurch Catholics also became less obvious.

Anticlerical liberals and prochurch Catholics had less to hold them together as the Dutch threat faded in the late 1830s. In particular, liberal antiunionism took shape in the face of evidence that liberal freedoms were aiding the church. The antiunionist opposition was sparked, for example, by the 1834 founding of the Catholic University at Louvain; liberals founded their own Free University in Brussels in 1836. In this and similar cases, liberals charged that the church was taking advantage of constitutional compromises to impose clerical rule. Political Catholics claimed that liberals, in their attempt to secularize authority in various institutions, were themselves violating the initial compromise on religious issues.

---

1. This may have been the view of industrialists in urban areas as late as 1866 (Gubin and Lefèvre 1985, 333). See also Puissant 1982, 157–59.

Liberals outside of government agitated for a break with the union and the prochurch politicians. In preparation for the elections of 1836, and especially those of 1839, liberals established party organizations in principal cities. Some of this rapid party development rested on the preexisting structure of Masonic lodges, which became increasingly politicized by church condemnation in 1838. Democrats and young radicals also swelled the ranks of party activists. The formation of election committees was accompanied by the foundation of liberal newspapers. All of these developments surpassed the organization among political Catholics:

> Although the Catholic camp sought to compete with its own newspapers, liberals enjoyed, in this area, an advantage that they would maintain for a long time. Anticlericals succeeded in creating a political organization adapted to the urban elector, which permitted them to win electoral victories. (Witte and Craeybeckx 1987, 39)

Much of this organization took place outside of parliament, as leading parliamentary liberals were still engaged in the politics of unionism with the Catholic political leaders.

Liberals took an important step in the drive to end unionism when they formed a national organization to mobilize voters. The Liberal Congress of 1846 was the first time that like-minded politicians met from around a country for the explicit purpose of forming a permanent, extraparliamentary organization to nominate candidates and organize voters. Belgian liberals, in other words, were the first Europeans to attempt to build this crucial aspect of a modern political party.

The evidence that anticlericalism formed the most important element of newly organized Belgian liberalism is clear. Anticlericalism occupied the central position of the official program of liberalism approved by the first Congress of the Liberal Party in 1846. Articles two and three of this program called for "true independence of civil authority" and for the "organization of public education at all levels." Public education was to be provided with "constitutional means of maintaining competition against private [Catholic] establishments" and was to eliminate "intervention by ministers of cults in the name of civil authority in the education organized by civil authority." During the congress itself there was no dissension on these anticlerical articles or on the posture adopted toward the church generally. In fact, delegates to the congress spent virtually the entire session, 9:30 A.M. to 3:30 P.M., discussing two matters that divided liberals among themselves, namely the party's positions on franchise expansion and social reform (Congrès Libéral de Belgique

1846). Right from the beginnings of an organized liberal party, liberals were united on anticlerical matters and divided on issues of equality.

Foreign observers recognized the frankly anticlerical program of the Liberal party. A Parisian journal reported the 1846 Congress in these terms:

> The flagrant battle for the past five years between the Catholic party and the Liberal party has just produced an extremely important event. . . . It was decided that a liberal congress would meet in Brussels. . . . The assembly adopted . . . a plan for the general confederation of all the liberals of Belgium, and a program that will henceforth serve as the basis for all candidacies and for the parliamentary conduct of elected candidates. We do not need to say that in all of this it is a matter of combating the influence of the clergy in politics, public education and administration.[2]

The anticlerical articles were central not just in the 1846 program of liberalism but also in the program of liberalism throughout the remainder of the century. Revisions of the program in 1870 and 1894 did not touch anticlericalism; the only articles amended were, again, those dealing with issues such as the proper extent of the franchise and amelioration of the condition of the working class (See Lefèvre 1989, 75–76). Anticlericalism was linked rhetorically by liberal pamphleteers to other liberal goals, such as constitutional and parliamentary government. But the fact remains that anticlericalism was the central unifying tenet for liberals in Belgium. Liberalism in Belgium came to be synonymous with opposition to the influence of the Catholic Church in government.

Liberal attitudes toward the church hardened over time. The official view of liberals at the congress of 1846 was that Rome dominated a reluctant clergy: "The liberal congress hopes for the emancipation by all legal means of the lower clergy, which is under the constant threat of dismissal and whose civil constitution is violated with impunity" (Congrès Libéral 1846, 64). Since the lower clergy were seen as fundamentally opposed to foreign authority, parish priests deserved liberal support. In introducing the above proposition, M. Forgeur from Liége said, "It seems to me that the Congress cannot adjourn without having given this proof of sympathy for the lower clergy" (my translation). The congress's resolution was the last major sympathetic view of the lower clergy. In the period after 1846, liberals viewed the lower clergy as more loyal to Rome and the episcopate than to Brussels and liberalism.

The anticlericalism of the Belgian liberals illustrates a basic aspect of continental European liberalism that can only be overlooked by an exclusively

---

2. *L'Illustration, journal universel* 7, no. 175 (July 4, 1846): 275.

Anglo-American perspective. Anticlericalism was common in Catholic Europe and its advocates were nominally still Catholics even if they rejected the authority of clergy. Anticlericalism as a phenomenon had its own history with roots, like liberalism, in the seventeenth and eighteenth centuries (Rémond 1976). The anticlericalism of the Belgian liberal movement can be understood as an instance of a more general pattern: a social movement will take an anticlerical position if individual and societal secularization are at odds, that is, if the members of a social movement are relatively secularized at an individual level (they do not accept the authority of clergy over their life choices) even as societal secularization is not far advanced (the clergy exercises authority through important social and political institutions such as education and the law) (Chaves 1994). For these historical and theoretical reasons, Belgian liberalism's early success cannot be understood without taking into account liberalism's aim of transforming the institutional links between church and state.

Liberal Dominance, Division, and Decline: 1847–84

We can now turn to the conditions for liberal dominance in the middle years of the century and the conditions allowed for the ultimate decline in liberal power. In terms of their ability to form governments, Belgian liberals were extraordinarily successful during the period of elite politics. Nowhere else on the Continent—with the exception of Switzerland, as we shall see—did liberals exercise as much power in national government as they did in Belgium. With the triumph over unionism in 1846, liberals became the dominant parliamentary fraction from 1847 to 1884. Liberals formed the government for 28 of these 37 years, while political Catholics formed the governments for only the remaining nine years.

Outside of government, liberals were far ahead of Catholics in mobilizing support among a restricted electorate. Both extraparliamentary organization and a narrow franchise were critical to liberal dominance. The social basis of liberalism, determined on the basis of ecological data, was predominantly the urban bourgeoisie, especially in Brussels, and some peasants in Wallonie (Bartier 1981 [1968]).

Yet the years of dominance were marked by divisions within the Liberal party itself, with the main division on the issue of equality. Doctrinaire and progressive factions took opposing sides in this debate. Doctrinaire liberals championed inequality, defended the restrictions on the franchise, and upheld the rights of employers. Progressives backed equality, sought to expand the franchise, and advocated worker protection. Doctrinaire and progressive politicians were not the only liberal elites who differed on socioeconomic issues. Liberal economists in Belgium were far ahead of many politicians in terms of promoting state intervention in the marketplace through child and female labor laws (Gubin and Lefèvre 1985). This much of the conflict in Belgium between the doctrinaires and the progressives was typical of struggles within liberal movements (elsewhere it appeared as a conflict between socially conservative liberals and radical liberals).

The leader of the parliamentary fraction of doctrinaire liberals, Walther Frère-Orban, declared that an expansion of the franchise would lead to the triumph of the clerical party and the downfall of liberalism (Van Leynseele and Garsou 1954, 71). Frère-Orban's fear of a democratic suffrage was inseparable from his estimation of the Catholic masses and their supposed obedience to ecclesiastic authority. Progressive liberals had a different program, namely that of revising Article 47 of the constitution to relax franchise limits. In the words of their leader, Paul Janson:

> If you want to replace the privilege of the minimum tax requirement with a more just regime, if you want to strengthen the bonds between bourgeois and worker, if you want the reform of our tariff system, if you want no one to be able to shirk the duty of defending our country, if you want to check the excesses of clerical tyranny, if you want public education to have a strong and robust organization, if, in a word, you want a broad, generous and democratic system . . . then enlist yourself under the banner of revision.[3]

Doctrinaire liberals, along with political Catholics, rejected efforts to broaden the franchise, notably by defeating Janson's 1883 proposal in parliament by 116 to 11 with 6 abstentions (Delange-Janson 1962, 289).

Much of the story of liberalism revolves around a central irony regarding the relative strengths of the two liberal factions. Doctrinaire liberals dominated the parliamentary faction of the party (the 1883 split giving 55 seats to the doctrinaires and just seven to the progressives was typical). This extreme imbalance in elected officials reflected the predilection of the narrow electorate. Among the politically active but disenfranchised, however, the progressives gained strength quickly. Progressives organized massive public demonstrations in the larger urban areas, notably in Brussels. Doctrinaires controlled government, but progressives seemed ascendant in urban society.

---

3. Paul Janson, speech of June 12, 1885 at Mons, in Delange-Janson 1962, 346 (my translation).

A second irony made the imbalances between doctrinaire and progressive factions debilitating in Belgium: neither liberal faction developed a strong organization in the countryside. Progressive plans for franchise expansion threatened to allow the Catholic party to develop this type of support to the detriment of liberals generally. Yet intransigence by doctrinaires, given their weakness among urban masses, was an equally untenable position in the long run.

How could liberals answer the question of franchise expansion without handing power to a Catholic party? This question posed an especially sharp dilemma because there were the beginnings of Catholic political organization. Liberals faced an opposition in part because liberals themselves had provided the conditions for its growth. The Belgian Catholic party, operating within a parliamentary system, was the first religiously based political party in Europe. Catholics adopted several liberal ideas, notably on constitutional government and economic freedom. The early development of liberalism and the encouragement of a Catholic opposition increased the challenge to liberalism as the era of mass politics approached.

Thus, the question facing the Liberal party in the run-up to the election of 1878 was how the threat of Catholic opposition could be neutralized. How could the franchise be expanded without conceding electoral victory to the Catholic party? Liberals developed several answers to this question, all of which ultimately relied on the secularizing influence of education. As we shall see in the coming analysis, strong rural reaction to the liberals' secularizing program for education and then the elites' conceding of defeat ended the era of liberal dominance.

One strategic answer to the problem of how to expand the franchise in the presence of a Catholic peasantry was to expand the franchise unevenly. As progressive leaders typically advocated, one could enfranchise only the *capacitaires,* those who had the capacity to exercise good judgment. Capacity was to be measured by having attained a certain level of formal education. Although ultimately not adopted per se, the strategy of restricting the franchise to those who were likely to vote liberal remained an important element of the liberal formula. When universal male suffrage was finally adopted in 1893, for example, the law gave additional votes to holders of certain higher education diplomas (Barthélemy 1912; Hill 1974).

Doctrinaire leaders favored another strategy for combining an expanded franchise and a Catholic peasantry, and this was the solution that was put into practice: attempt to change the sympathies of the countryside *before* expanding the franchise. The plan was to remove the countryside from the supposed thrall of the Catholic Church by providing the youth with secular education. As one prominent liberal put it, "happily, liberals have finally understood . . . the necessity of conquering future generations, which they will do insofar as the battle is pressed on religious terrain."[4] Or again, "Liberty is the essence of our Constitution. Public education will raise children in liberty; it will thereby become the strongest guarantee of our institutions and our nationality."[5]

Secular education required major changes in the education system. Religious instruction was mandatory in state primary schools, and in regions where the church was strong, as in most of the countryside, the clergy had veto power over all other elements of the curriculum and over the hiring and firing of the instructors themselves. The Liberal party's new 1879 Law on Education required each local administration to establish at least one secular school. Religion was to be removed from the curriculum and instructors were required to have diplomas from state institutes of education. The gravity of this educational policy was not lost on liberals:

> Even limiting its mission during the first years [in power] to the development and secularization of public instruction, the liberal government will have to make long and energetic efforts. Its task, of which we must hide from ourselves neither the grandeur nor the difficulties, will not however be beyond its power if it finds within the Liberal party the unanimous and confident support to which it has the right.[6]

This policy was virtually the only program that could unite doctrinaire and progressive factions, for it emphasized their shared anticlericalism.

The prospect of declining support for the party and the lack of any other shared program pushed liberals toward an ambitious program for educational reform (Lefèvre 1989, 81–82). The doctrinaire plan to secularize education was the strategy chosen at least in part because the Liberal party was mainly united—to the extent that it was united—by the desire to laicize education and the state. Outside of the agreement on anticlericalism, as we have seen, the

---

4. Goblet d'Alviela, in the *Revue de Belgique* 25 (February 15, 1877): 216 (my translation). D'Alviela was a thoroughgoing anticlerical himself and the anticlerical position was ascendant when he wrote these lines in 1877. A November 15, 1878, article in the *Revue* (signed by the editorial committee: Alb. Callier, Laveleye, D'Alviella, and Ch. Potvin, among others) outlined the journal's mission as anticlericalism, ascribed the 1878 electoral victory to this position, and asserted that the first task of liberalism was educational reform.

5. F. Laurent, "La Loi de 1842," *Revue de Belgique,* November 15, 1878, 237 (my translation).

6. Albert Callier, "L'Élection du 11 juin 1878," *Revue de Belgique,* July 15, 1878, 242 (my translation).

party was strongly divided into doctrinaire, moderate, progressive and radical factions for most of the mass period. Although doctrinaire liberal opinion was the dominant force in government, this force was never matched by the growth of a party organization to support it. The party did not acquire strong central organization and congresses of members were infrequent (there were just three congresses from 1846 to 1910).

The consequences of the liberal strategies in the context of expanding participation in the 1870s and 1880s were not favorable to the party's electoral fortunes. Belgian liberals, like most of Europe's liberals, still enjoyed the support of the urban elite. An important cause of variation lay in the relationship of these urban liberals to social groups in the countryside. Given the narrow support for anticlericalism, Belgian liberals feared the clerical sympathies of the mass of the peasantry. Liberals sought to overcome the obstacle of rural clericalism in two ways: First, Belgian liberals maintained Europe's most restrictive franchise requirements in order to prevent the Catholic peasantry from having a formal say in national politics. Second, they attacked the church's role in education. Liberals intended the new, secular education system to free future voters from the influence of the clergy.

Unfortunately for Belgian liberals, promoting secular education undermined strict limits on political participation. Most importantly, the attack on the church's privileges in education provoked an unprecedented reaction of defense from the countryside from 1879 to 1884. Parents were politically organized well before their children could be educated in the liberal creed. As liberals soon realized, the plan to secularize the electorate by eliminating the church from primary education did not succeed. Rather than secularize the youth, the Education Law of 1879 mobilized the hitherto politically inactive parents into political action directed at the state. The spiral of intensifying political conflict between liberals and an increasingly organized Catholic sector was largely unplanned and unintentional, especially among the latter (Kalyvas 1996, 171–221).

The liberal education policy sparked explosive growth in support for the Catholic party, especially in the countryside. Catholics in Flanders boycotted state schools, which the liberal government continued to build at considerable expense, even as the government cut financial support for the church. Parents, meanwhile, helped to finance and support new parochial institutions: in 1879 just 379,000 students attended Catholic primary schools, just three years later in 1882, fully 622,000 children did so (Kossmann 1978, 362). The school struggle also provoked the founding of formal political organizations, such as the Union nationale pour le redressement des griefs, which reshaped political

Catholicism in the direction of more active opposition to liberalism and less compromise (Kossmann 1978, 364).

The Catholic reaction to the liberal program for primary education made for a liberal defeat in the elections of 1884. Liberals lost their ability to win elections, even among a restricted electorate, beginning in the election of 1884. The different social bases of the Liberal and Catholic parties in the elections of 1884 were illustrated by the difference in the presentation of statistics by the two parties. A Catholic leader, Jules Malou, presented the results of the communal elections of 1884 by comparing the percentage of local officials elected from the Catholic party to the percentage of local officials elected from the Liberal party (Malou [1884]). His calculations showed that just 40.49 percent of officials were liberal, while 59.51 percent were Catholic, excluding a substantial number of officials classified as neutral. The Liberal party responded with its own presentation, based on the same data, which took into account the size of the population represented by each communal official.[7] The liberal calculation compared the percentage of the population represented by liberals to the percentage of the population represented by Catholics. Liberals represented 48.08 percent, Catholics 41.88 percent and neutrals represented 10.04 percent of the population according to the liberal figures. The difference between these two sets of calculations reveals more than just the fact that statistics are the third type of lie. The difference in the calculation preferred by the parties reflected the strength of the Catholic party throughout the countryside, including many small communes with small populations, versus the strength of the Liberal party in many larger urban areas. Although ecological data are the only data available, they clearly show that liberals lost the communal election of 1884 by losing the vote in the smaller communities of the northern plain. Cities in the north—such as Ghent, Ostend and Antwerp—remained in liberal hands, as did Brussels and most of southern Belgium (Malou [1884]). The national election posed great problems for liberals.

The causes of the liberal defeat in 1884 were examined by liberal pamphleteers in the immediate aftermath. After considering grievances in other areas such as tariff policy, one pamphlet concluded, "Believe us, one can not hide the fact that the law of 1879 was the principal cause of the fall of the liberal ministry." Confessing that liberal leaders were out of touch with the temper of the countryside, the author remarked that "the voice of the last peasant in Flanders counts as much on election day as that of Monsieur Frère-

---

7. *Carte figurative des élections communales du 19 octobre 1884 dressée en réponse à la Carte de Monsieur J. Malou,* January 1885.

Orban" (*Le Dix Juin* 1884, 26). The liberals' attempt to secularize the future electorate failed so badly that the Catholic party was able to seize power even without franchise reform. The critical point is that liberals lost their support within even the restricted franchise; marginal liberal voters, when faced with growing opposition to the liberal program of laicization, turned away from their former party.

Why Did the Liberal Party Embark on a Suicidal Course?

What motivated the liberal government, elected by a bare majority in 1878, to enact a thoroughgoing reform in 1879? It was this election which ushered in the final four years of Liberal party government in Belgium. Liberals took this opportunity finally to attempt a broad overhaul of the system of primary education, even though this had been a central plank of the party's program since 1846. The margin of victory was slim: liberals enjoyed a majority of about 10 seats in the chamber and six seats in the senate. Yet on the basis of this slim electoral mandate the government embarked upon the most thoroughgoing reform of education in Belgian history by seeking to end clerical influence in state schools. With the benefit of hindsight, we know that this assault on the church provoked a backlash which swept the Catholic party to power (which it subsequently held uninterruptedly until World War II). What explains the liberals' final act in power?

Liberals miscalculated how far their mandate would carry them by interpreting their victory in a way that emphasized the role of liberal ideology. Liberals ascribed the victory to several causes, but foremost among them was the leadership of Frère-Orban. Frère-Orban's speech to the chamber in May of 1878 was widely seen as the rallying cry of liberal opinion. In that address, Frère-Orban called for the unity of the Liberal party on the issue of anticlericalism. Liberals may have overestimated the degree to which their victory was due to deep support for an anticlerical program.

But letters sent to Frère-Orban by his liberal colleagues show that liberals were not uniform in assessing the sympathies of the electorate after the election's bare margin of victory. Some indeed argued that the climate of opinion favored an increased majority if new elections were held, and thus counseled dissolving the chamber and calling new elections in the whole of the country. Calmer correspondents argued strongly against this position by citing the slim margin of victories in Bruges, Antwerp and other provinces in Flanders. On this view, new elections would open these bare victories to new challenges.

The decision to attack the church is even more perplexing, since liberals were aware that a portion, perhaps a decisive portion, of the electorate that had voted liberal in 1878 also had substantial allegiance to the church. This was evident in the correspondence that Frère-Orban received on what sort of program the new government should pursue. Paul Devaux cautioned against antagonizing the church precisely on the grounds that this would needlessly upset the "floating" electors who had Catholic sensibilities but had nevertheless voted for liberals.[8]

An important miscalculation of the liberals was in assessing the strategies the Catholic party would employ in resisting educational reform. Frère-Orban not only underestimated the popular reaction, but also and more importantly he misjudged the "game" the Catholics were playing. Rather than use popular opposition to force a change in the law, the Catholic party used popular opposition to force a change in the government itself. Simply put, the liberal ministry expected that Catholic deputies in the chamber of representatives would offer compromise amendments to the ministry's education proposal. The ministry would then be able to develop graciously a compromise proposal. The plan would have satisfied liberals by embarking on the reform of education and would have mollified Catholics through concessions. Liberal ministers made overtures to Catholics to the effect that amendments would be considered. But Catholic deputies did not play the part expected of them; they offered no amendments to the ministry's proposal (Frère-Orban 1879, 4–5).

Catholics left the liberal ministry free to adopt its complete education reform in parliament. Outside of parliament, however, Catholics organized massive resistance to the new schools. Parishes founded competing religious schools (where these were not already present) while enrollment at state schools plummeted. Opposition to school reform became the opportunity for Catholics to make up the organizational and mobilizational deficit that had plagued them since midcentury. Once in power, the new Catholic cabinet won parliamentary approval for a new education law to end central control of schools; under the new system, local communities could adopt or subsidize Catholic schools, and the state relinquished control of teaching methods, curriculum content, and teacher training (Kossmann 1978, 367).

Despite model beginnings during the unionist period (1830–46) and nearly four decades of dominance (1847–84), the Liberal party in the latter part of the nineteenth century stood in danger of vanishing as a political force. After

---

8. This advice was offered in the context of foreign policy, especially Belgium's official relations with the Vatican. The king, the queen, Paul Devaux, and others warned against withdrawing official recognition of the Holy See. One must emphasize the importance that foreign policy toward the Vatican held in the nineteenth century.

losing the turning-point election of 1884, liberals never again topped 50 percent of the vote. Support for the Liberal party dwindled to 11 percent of the vote by 1912.[9] Liberals formed no government after 1884.

Failed Attempts to Reinvigorate a Liberal Coalition: 1884–1914

The decline of liberal institutions took place primarily in government, education policy, and the privileges of the Catholic Church. In government, the Catholic party formed cabinets with parliamentary majorities from 1884 to World War I. Even such continued parliamentary presence as the liberals did enjoy depended upon Catholic forbearance (through proportional representation and multiple votes for the wealthy). Once in power, the Catholic party rewrote liberal education laws to give the Catholic Church control of primary education in most of Belgium. As for political rights, franchise expansion lagged behind most of the rest of Europe, with most adult men receiving the right to vote only in 1893. As for labor, about half of Belgium's industrial workers engaged in general strikes in 1893, 1902, and 1913 (Kossmann 1978, 508 n. 2).

Under conservative government, ironically, the Liberal party was saved from extinction by the grace of the Catholic party. Liberal fortunes depended upon how the Catholic party handled franchise questions: introducing universal suffrage in 1893 nearly eliminated the liberals, but the law preserved liberals through plural voting rights until 1914; Catholics gave an additional lease on life to the Liberal party by changing to proportional representation in 1899. Catholics extended suffrage rights broadly, which hurt the liberals, but Catholics sought to do so in a manner that would prevent a straight fight between themselves and the emerging Socialist party.

The combination of plural voting with universal suffrage, which pertained between 1894 and 1919, was premised on a belief that those with more wealth and education were more likely to vote liberal than those with less. A second major shift in electoral institutions took place in the way votes were translated into seats. The majoritarian system of tallying votes in each commune and awarding the parliamentary seat to each winner worked to the detriment of the Liberal party, whose electors were not as concentrated in a few districts as those of the Socialist party. In 1894, the liberals gained 20 seats with about 550,000 votes (including votes for progressive and socialist cartels), whereas the socialists gained more seats, 28, with fewer votes, about 330,000. The governing Catholic party introduced the system of proportional representation

---

9. For election statistics, see Mackie and Rose 1991.

to preserve the Liberal party (Stengers 1989), thus inaugurating one of the crucial institutions that ensures a "fair distribution of power" in a consociational system (Lijphart 1981, 8).

Catholics introduced proportional representation both to avoid being left alone against the socialists and to prevent the formation of cartels between socialists and liberals (Stengers 1989). On the first count of preserving liberals, the aims of the Catholics were met, with the liberals rebounding in the election of 1900 with 25 percent of the vote and 22 percent of parliamentary seats from the previous 1898 result of 19 percent of the vote and just 9 percent of seats (Flora 1983b, 103, 158). On the second count of preventing a cartel, however, the aims of the Catholics were not met: liberals and socialists waged the campaign of 1912 on the basis of a cartel.

The cartel of 1912 revealed more than the failure of a proportional representation system to prevent electoral agreements between parties. Its results more fundamentally showed how the clerical/anticlerical cleavage divided the Belgian electorate and gave the proclerical side a majority position. Cartels were not entirely new, having played a role in Belgium in 1906. But the 1912 cartel was a broad, concerted effort: liberals and socialists presented common lists in twenty-five of thirty constituencies. The highest levels of both parties authorized the cartel, as the liberal leader, Paul Hymans, and the socialist leader, Émile Vandervelde, underscored by holding a joint campaign rally in Brussels.

What did the parties seek to gain from the cartel? The aim of the cartel was to wrest power from the Catholic party, which had had a twenty-eight year run of uninterrupted power since 1884. What was the program of the liberal-socialist cartel? The election was fought squarely on the anticlerical issue. The 1884 education law had been replaced with a system that strengthened Catholic authority in primary education and the Catholic cabinet proposed in 1911 an even greater state grant to Catholic schools (Kossmann 1978, 506–7). Liberal and socialist candidates had performed well in communal elections in the fall of 1911 and expected to succeed in the general election of June 1912.

The result of the election, however, was not a gain for the liberals and socialists. Instead, the Catholic party gained both in votes and in seats in the assembly and the campaign was ultimately unsuccessful in overturning the Catholic majority. The cartel's failure to overturn the Catholic majority has been interpreted as revealing many liberal voters' fear of the socialists. Despite the instructions of party leaders, in other words, many liberal voters preferred a clerical regime to one that included socialists (Stengers 1989). Socialist and liberal programs were thought to be sufficiently disparate to prevent a majority of Belgians from supporting the aims of both.

The inability of the anticlerical issue to bridge the increasingly divisive socioeconomic questions among liberals has been seen in the failure of the 1912 cartel; it can also be traced in the writings of a prominent liberal thinker. The Comte Goblet D'Alviella was a prolific liberal publicist noted for his hostility to the church. D'Alviella's main goal throughout the period of his activity—he published pamphlets from the early 1870s through World War I—was the unity of the Liberal party. But there is an important change over this period as the problems facing the Liberal party changed. In the 1870s, the party was faced mainly with the external opposition of the Catholic party and the internal quarrel of the radicals and the doctrinaires. To overcome internal dissension as well as the external enemy in this period, D'Alviella recommended a reliance on a thoroughgoing anticlerical program. Anticlericalism would be the common program to overcome the divisions provoked by franchise and economic issues. By the turn of the century, the party was faced with a double opposition, their old enemies the Catholics on the one hand and the newly emerged Socialist party on the other. The internal strife between doctrinaire and radical had given way to a new struggle between a reduced Liberal party and a new Socialist party. The old tactic of thoroughgoing anticlericalism no longer seemed reasonable to D'Alviella. An anticlerical program, in a joint effort with the Socialist party, was not, D'Alviella argued, in the interest of the Liberal party. Liberals should not compromise on economic issues in order to win the active support of socialists on the religious front. Anticlericalism was no longer adequate to bridge the socioeconomic cleavage. Between 1874 and 1900 it became increasingly difficult to bridge the political expression of the socioeconomic cleavage through anticlericalism.

The cartel's failure convinced socialists and liberals of the need to act independently (Stengers 1989). Socialists opted for a general strike in 1913 in order to attain universal suffrage without provisions for plural voting; socialist leaders later advised socialists elsewhere—particularly, in the Netherlands—to learn from the Belgian example and avoid a common cartel with liberals. As for the liberals, Paul Hymans wrote in December of 1912, "one must proclaim the necessity for the Liberal party to indicate in all circumstances its autonomy to assert its personality. We must make apparent the traits belonging to liberalism alone" (Stengers 1989, 118). These were the remarks of the same Paul Hymans who had shared the tribune with the socialist leader just a few months before and who had been expected to lead a liberal-socialist cabinet.

In emphasizing anticlericalism as the common element in liberal and socialist programs, the Belgian cartel of 1912 echoed a campaign of six years before in France. In both cases, campaign strategy brought together the disparate forces of the left mainly on the issue of ending the Catholic Church's involvement in education. Anticlericalism could be an effective strategy under certain conditions, for French Republicans, Radicals and Socialists emphasized anticlericalism and won the elections in 1906. In fact, French liberal forces had repeatedly triumphed by emphasizing religious questions in the late nineteenth and early twentieth centuries. The next chapter explores why religious institutions and liberal reform interacted differently in France.

Conclusion

How can the early and late contributions of religious issues to Belgian politics be reconciled? The initial elite compromise among political Catholics and anticlerical liberals rested on the shared drive for independence. Belgian liberalism enjoyed a special advantage under elite politics, a strong state-building issue encouraging elites to seek accommodation on otherwise divisive religious issues. The initial compromise set in motion a chain of events that undermined the liberal-Catholic compromise in the long run. The specific events in the chain involved the contradictions between the liberals' attempts to strengthen liberal institutions and the Catholics' attempts to take advantage of liberal freedoms. As a result, the institutions built with the aid of the initial compromise between liberals and their opponents had unforseen consequences no less important than a revival of popular Catholic religiosity. Many liberals became concerned about the influence of the Catholic Church and sought to secularize the state and its relationship to society. Unfortunately for the electoral fortunes of the Liberal party, the program of forced secularization drove a wedge between the liberal candidates and the Catholic constituency and sparked the formation of a new mass organization of political Catholicism.

Comparing two periods of time within a single country shows that the conditions for liberal success in one era were different from the conditions for success in a later era. In the elite period of nineteenth-century politics, the coalition necessary for building liberal institutions had to include not only urban, secular elites but also clergy and proclerical leaders. In Belgium, the secular-clerical coalition central to elite liberalism was facilitated by shared interests on the issue of independence from the Netherlands. In the mass period, however, the coalition had to reach deeper into mass sympathies and incorporate provincial middle classes and peasants. In this expanded realm, liberals confronted proclerical attitudes in the countryside, and, most importantly, a growing set of organizations committed to the defense of the church. Liberals attempted to transform proclerical attitudes before franchise expansion, as we have seen, through an aggressive program of secularizing primary education. Educational reform, however, encouraged the Catholic opposition to organize a broader response to liberal programs and even deepen the proclerical sentiment of the mass of the peasantry. In the period of mass politics, then, liberal dominance was not possible in the presence of organized rural proclericalism.

As for Belgian politics after 1884, the foregoing developments led to the persistence of a basically liberal regime, modified by substantial reserved powers for the Catholic Church, the Catholic party's predominance in electoral politics, and the reliance on procedures for power-sharing. From 1884 to World War I, liberals lost their previously dominant position completely and the Catholic party won every election and formed every government. Following World War I, Catholic parties anchored coalition governments of the center-left and center-right (Wilensky 1981, 364). The pattern of power-sharing intensified after World War II as a grand coalition of liberals, Catholics, and socialists negotiated the 1958 School Pact that awarded each of the three a large measure of autonomy, laying down a further component of a fully consociational system (Lijphart 1981, 12). Thus was Belgian liberalism defeated, albeit only partially and with important conditions.

The interaction of institutions, liberal initiatives, clerical responses, and the dynamics of reform underline the distinctive contribution of nineteenth-century religious institutions to twentieth-century outcomes. As we have seen, the decisive contribution of religion to the fate of Belgian liberalism began with the very founding of the Belgian state under a liberal regime in 1830 and continued through the electoral defeat of the Liberal party in 1884. Highlighting these aspects of Belgian political change parallels renewed scholarly efforts to fill in the intervening steps between preindustrial patterns and their legacies in Belgian politics (Strikwerda 1997). As this chapter has argued, religious institutions shaped modern politics neither merely as holdovers from the past nor only where industrial modernization had not yet taken hold. Instead, religious institutions animated reform attempts as well as creative new attempts to promote religious authority. Clerical and political leaders sympathetic to the Catholic Church found ways to draw strength from reforms initiated by liberals.

Chapter 3

Failed Reform and Contested Victory in France

France had an intermediate outcome with respect to the fate of liberal parties and type of regime. Liberal reforms in the elite phase of politics were not sustained even though they took place within an environment that in many ways favored liberal outcomes. In 1815 Louis XVIII agreed to set out the framework of his rule in a written charter as a condition of the restoration of the monarchy, thus steering a course between a full-scale return to the old regime and a thorough acceptance of liberal constitutionalism. While the charter asserted monarchical sovereignty and the king's virtually unlimited discretion in selecting ministers, the acceptance of the Napoleonic Civil Code, an elected assembly, and the revolutionary land transfers marked significant departures from prerevolutionary absolutism. Even more than in the realm of politics, in economics and in social relations the so-called Restoration did not represent a total reversal of liberalism. Yet the monarchy turned decisively conservative in the 1820s, abjured further liberalism, and fell to revolution. A new constitutional monarchy emerged with a clear acceptance of liberal principles in 1830. This was France's first truly liberal regime; it had clear practices of constitutional and representative government and even strong tendencies to distinguish between political and religious authority. Yet this constitutional monarchy also turned to the right and collapsed in revolution, this time in February of 1848. When a series of elections in 1848–51 revealed limited support for liberal candidates, many erstwhile liberals deserted constitutionalism to support the authoritarian coup of Louis Napoleon in 1851. The failure of the liberal movement to maintain a successful constitutional monarchy requires some explanation. In other words, if the Restoration enshrined some liberal principles, and if economic and social developments favored many forces generally supportive of liberalism thereafter, why did attempts at reform fail to take hold?

In the wake of Louis Napoleon's defeat in war and a domestic uprising in 1870, liberals founded the Third Republic. This second great attempt to sustain a liberal regime enshrined basic liberal principles of constitutional government. Liberalism developed support across the broad middle of the political spectrum. On the center-left, the Republican party, while somewhat to the left of most other European liberals, adopted the three main elements of liberalism: constitutional and representative government, free markets, and distinctions between political and religious authority. The party also dominated electoral returns throughout the duration of the Republic. The regime faced repeated threats, both electoral and nonconstitutional, from aristocrats, pretenders to the throne, and the army. Still, the Republic, ultimately under a Popular Front government, ended only with the German invasion in 1940. Notwithstanding the earlier experiences of short-lived constitutional monarchies and republics, why did the Third Republic survive as long as it did?

A comparison of the two great attempts to sustain liberal regimes in France, the constitutional monarchy of 1830–48 and the Third Republic of 1870–1940, provides material for examining the interaction among institutions, reform dynamics, and political outcomes. This chapter proceeds by first considering the role of economic development in explaining differences between these two regimes. While economic development cannot be ignored, the evidence presented here cautions against making it the sole or even the primary explanation of the differences between these regimes. Second, the chapter turns to examining the prior institutions, liberal reform, and reform dynamics that underlie the attempts to sustain liberal regimes. A section on the monarchy of 1830–48 corresponds to the elite phase of politics in the overall argument and a section on the Third Republic of 1870–1940 corresponds to the mass phase.

Socioeconomic Development

Differing levels of economic development only partly account for the differences between the July Monarchy and the Third Republic. Industrialization did add to the resources available to France under the Third Republic. According to a leading index, France's per capita industrialization was just 17 under the constitutional monarchy in 1840; by the time of the crucial national election in support of a liberal constitution for the Third Republic in 1877 the index had climbed to 25.[1] French industrialization involved the development of railroads, newspapers, and other forms of rapid communication to the extent that Eugen Weber argues that they helped forge a single national community with values that supported the Third Republic (1976). Industrial elites favored the Third Republic and helped support the regime's leading political party (Elwitt 1975; Lebovics 1988).

---

1. Interpolated from estimated triennial annual average per capita levels of industrialization, where 100 represents the level of per capita industrialization in the United Kingdom in 1900 (Bairoch 1982, 294, 330).

TABLE 4. Institutions, Reform Dynamics, and Outcomes in France

Elite Phase

State and Church Institutions at Onset of Liberal Reform	*Non-liberal, incorporated church* Neo-absolutist Catholic monarch allied to Catholic Church by 1815 Restoration
Liberal policy toward Religious Authority	*Attack* Curtail Catholic Church authority in 1830 Revolution
Response of Clergy	*Opposition* Defeat proliberal clergy of Lamennaisian movement, ally with monarch, aristocrats, and conservative deputies
Fate of Elite Liberal Reform	**Failed** Monarch and constitutions fall to 1848 Revolution

Mass Phase

Institutions at Onset of Second Liberal Reform	*Emperor sovereign* Authoritarian Empire of Louis Napoleon (1852–70) allied to Catholic Church
Liberal Policy toward Religious Authority	*Attack* Criticize and curtail church authority in education and other public institutions
Response of Clergy	*Opposition* Clergy support emperor, aristocrats, pretenders, Boulanger, and anti-Dreyfusards
Provincial Middle-Class and Peasant Reply	*Support liberals* Peasants in south-east and provincial middle classes accept mobilization by Republicans and Radicals
Party and Regime Outcome	**Contested Victory of Liberals** *Strong liberal party in a contested constitutional democracy* Republicans and Radicals dominate Third Republic (1870s–1940) despite repeated anti-systemic challenges

As important as economic development was, it was not the whole story. France's level of gross domestic product did not rule out the possibility of failure for the Third Republic. In comparative perspective, countries that attained similar and even higher levels of economic development had a mixed record in sustaining liberal regimes. France inaugurated the Third Republic when at a relatively low level of per capita gross domestic product: $1,858 in 1870.[2] Italy and Germany inaugurated liberal democracies in 1919 at the higher levels of $2,783 and $2,763, respectively. France also sustained its democracy at modest levels of gross domestic product per capita, reaching $2,734 only in 1898. The democratic regimes in Italy and Germany fell at the comparable or higher levels of $2,703 in 1923 and $3,591 in 1933, respectively. Nor is economic development the whole story if one wishes to understand the shift from the religious conservatism of the late constitutional monarchy to the secularizing policies of the Third Republic in the 1880s. Political regimes in Belgium and the Netherlands gave substantial powers to religious institutions, yet these countries had even higher levels of per capita gross domestic product than France, both $3,000 in the 1880s.

Several causal mechanisms that scholars have proposed as the links between socioeconomic development and liberalism did not operate as expected in France. For Seymour Martin Lipset, the middle class is a crucial agent translating societal wealth into political contestation. Yet the French middle classes often supported authoritarian rule; as Marx argued, French middle classes in 1851 exchanged the right to rule for the right to make money (1977 [1852], 67). For Dietrich Rueschemeyer, Evelyne Huber Stephens, and John D. Stephens, the working class is the most consistently prodemocratic force, yet their analysis of the French case confirms that the working classes pushed for reform in advance of what other social classes desired, especially with regard to economic policy (1992, 89). The leading scholarly approaches to understanding France thus open up the possibility that other factors besides the class interests of the middle classes or workers as such were critical to the advancement of liberal democracy.

Constitutional Monarchy Attempted, 1830–48

The constitutional monarchy matched the main ideals of liberalism at the time. The Chamber of Deputies wielded more power than it had under the preceding restored Bourbon monarchy (1815–30). Even as the chamber acclaimed the

---

2. Per capita gross domestic product figures in this paragraph are in terms of 1990 Geary-Khamis dollars as found in Maddison 1995, 194–96.

new king, Louis Philippe of Orleans, they amended the Charter of 1814 to limit royal power: the king henceforth had to share lawmaking authority with the chamber and no longer had the right to exercise emergency authority. Louis Philippe appointed several ministers he disliked and rarely opposed leading figures (Collingham 1988, 148–49). All of the ministries of the July Monarchy won majority support in the Chamber of Deputies. Political actors expected elections to take place with a degree of regularity into the indefinite future, which is a central feature of a liberal regime, and in fact elections were held about every three years.

The regime was largely undemocratic. The undemocratic aspects of the regime could be seen in the narrowness of what Robert Dahl labels participation (1971). In 1831, only 166,583 men paid the 200 francs per year in property taxes that qualified them for the franchise (2.8 percent of men over 21 or 0.5 percent of the population). In the early 1830s, few liberals expressed any strong support for extending the franchise; in fact, many liberals helped to stifle the emerging republican and democratic movements by 1834 (McPhee 1992, 53). As incomes increased over time, the ranks of the enfranchised grew only marginally to 240,983 (0.7 percent of the population) by the elections of 1846.[3] The regime also lacked some institutional attributes of modern democracies. The fluidity of political groups in the chamber allowed the king to influence cabinet formation; the majorities supporting cabinets were variable and usually small.

French liberalism's failure to consolidate the regime of 1830 can be traced to the interaction between liberalism and religious institutions. A potentially liberal movement within the Catholic Church was crushed by the upper hierarchy. The reinvigorated church reinforced conservative forces within the government and helped to derail any attempts to pursue further liberal and democratic reforms.

The post–1815 Restoration in France had placed the Catholic Church and the state in a mutually supportive position. A perennial question is why political Catholicism in France repeatedly supported monarchical authoritarianism; sympathetic scholars present this pattern in a tragic light (Weill 1909, 28ff; Moody 1966; Bressolette 1984). The institutional grounding for the church's role was laid down during the Restoration. The Charter declared apostolic Roman Catholicism to be the official religion of the state of France; a formal declaration of religious toleration also implied government supervision of the small Protestant and Jewish communities. During the 1820s the more reaction-

---

3. Among the many franchise figures in the literature, those cited in the text appear in Collingham 1988, 71, Cobban 1981 [1957], 2:98, and McPhee 1992, 54.

ary potential in the restoration arrangements developed even further as all levels of education came under clerical control and sacrilege became a civil crime. In 1824, the crowning of Charles X at the cathedral at Reims symbolically demonstrated the tightened connections between church and state. In this situation of mutual support, the church opposed liberalization in the 1820s and 1830s and offered crucial support to the most right-wing forces in the 1840s.

The possibility that the church would instead depart from its alliance with the crown was tested by a social and political movement led by a few radical clergy. The leader of the movement, Hugues-Félicité-Robert de Lamennais, began by publishing two early pamphlets prior to being ordained a priest in 1816. As a priest Lamennais published at an even greater rate and within his wide readership he attracted a devoted circle of associates in the 1810s and 1820s.

The main goal of Lamennais and his followers was to replace the French state's authority over the church with that of the pope. Such a goal placed Lamennais at odds with most of the upper hierarchy of the French church, who were enmeshed in the state-church relationship of mutual dependence. "Tonsured lackeys" is how Lamennais described high officials in the French church, "they are men who have no desire to act, but give them a kick in the appropriate place and you will find they have moved a hundred paces." (Dansette 1961 [1948], 1:214). An associate wrote that Lamennais "exerted more influence and possessed more authority over the younger clergy than did bishops and cardinals."[4] One of his enemies in the church hierarchy wrote that "the importance of the *Avenir* business [Lamennais's newspaper] should not be underestimated. The whole of the younger clergy is lost."[5]

The Lamennaisians reached the peak of their influence in the early years of the constitutional monarchy, that is, after the initial success of the Revolution of 1830. The revolution—and its anticlericalism—seemed to validate Lamennais's argument that Restoration-style ties between church and state did not help the church in the long run. An equally important effect of the Revolution of 1830 lay in the newly liberalized conditions for political organizing that the change of regime provided.

Lamennais's movement was not welcomed in the liberal camp for Lamennais was too populist, papist, and zealous for most liberals.[6] The Lamennaisian endorsement of universal suffrage placed the movement at odds with many propertied liberals; the emphasis on decentralization likewise ran counter to most liberal sympathies. Ironically, many of the viewpoints expressed in

---

4. Henri Lacordaire, cited in Reardon 1975, 107.
5. Abbé Dupanloup to the Cardinal de Rohan, cited in Dansette 1961 [1948], 1:220.
6. Philip Nord, personal communication, 1996.

L'Avenir are strikingly similar to early liberal views: liberty of conscience and religion, separation of church and state, freedom in education, freedom of the press, liberty of association. "One trembles before liberalism," wrote Lamennais, "well then, Catholicize it and society will be reborn." (Reardon 1975, 94–95, 90). At the end of 1830, Lamennais founded his explicitly political organization, the *Agence générale pour la défense de la liberté religieuse,* the stated mission of which was to defend the church against encroachment by the state. For example, in one of the organization's activities, Charles de Montalembert and Charles de Coux opened a Catholic school in 1831. While in other contexts the freedom to open a school might indicate a liberal regime, in this case opening a private school violated existing education laws and Montalembert was prosecuted.

Although the Lamennaisian movement surged in the moment of opportunity, it collapsed once the church hierarchy acted decisively against it. In a move that was more in line with his thinking than an alliance with liberals, Lamennais sought support from Rome. He and his two closest associates—Montalembert and fellow priest Henri Lacordaire—traveled to Rome to secure the pope's approval for their program of a newly rationalized church administration distinct from state institutions. They were bitterly disappointed. Pope Gregory XVI's encyclical *Mirari Vos* in 1832 condemned every aspect of the Lamennaisian doctrine: religious toleration, freedom of conscience, and the freedom of publication were each rejected. In a direct attack on the movement, the pope stated that priests were "forbidden by ancient canons to undertake ministry and to assume the tasks of teaching and preaching without the permission of their bishop." "All those who struggle against this established order," continued the pope, "disturb the position of the Church."[7] The encyclical asserted that the church was already sufficiently centralized in its structure of authority. Within a few months Lamennais spoke out against the pope and in 1834 he published another popular pamphlet, *Paroles d'un croyant,* that marked his final break with the church. He died without last rights or a Catholic burial in 1854. Few of Lamennais's adherents followed him on his final journey outside of the church.

What Lamennais's former followers did instead was signally important, for as priests they had institutional authority and could rise in the church hierarchy. Other figures, such as Flora Tristan, and other social movements with important religious aspects, such as Saint Simonianism, while important, played different roles as they did not have leaders in the church itself. In

---

7. "*Mirari Vos:* Encyclical of Pope Gregory XVI on Liberalism and Religious Indifferentism," August 15, 1832, paragraph 8. "*Singulari nos*" of 1834 continued the papal denunciation of the Lamennaisian doctrine.

analyzing phenomena such as these one must distinguish between organizational ties to a church on the one hand and the use of religious imagery on the other. Claire Goldberg Moses and Leslie Wahl Rabine do this when they write of the Saint Simonian feminists, "they created a 'new religion' that was to challenge traditional Christian theology and the organized Catholic Church, but their frequent reference to their 'word' or 'words' and their 'acts' and their self-representation as 'apostles' purposely reflects the early Christians" (1993, 8). Many movements are called to attach their principles to religious images and develop religious themes; few movements have leaders occupying positions in a durable clerical hierarchy.

Former followers of Lamennais rose to occupy key positions in the reunified national church. Lacordaire delivered a series of lecture-sermons, seventy-five addresses in all (in 1835, 1836, 1843–46, 1849, and 1850–51), mainly at Notre Dame in Paris, that drove home the theme of religious revival to large, predominantly elite, audiences (Boutry 1988, 429–30; Dansette 1961 [1948], 1:230–31). Seeking to further their goals of educational reform, former Lamennaisians in the 1840s forged an alliance with the conservative government. Montalembert in 1844 founded the *Comité électoral pour la défense de la liberté religieuse;* in 1845 he and his partners started to organize the Catholic electorate, among other ways by publishing an electors' guide explaining the law on enfranchisement; and in 1846 they published a series of pamphlets, including the successful *Du devoir des Catholiques dans les prochaines élections* (Johnson 1963, 217). The organizational capacity of the church to provide electoral support in an elite franchise made the church an attractive ally to the government.

Guizot's rejection of "the idea of a social or political seat of power, of any human depository of sovereignty" indicates his distance from liberalism; by attacking popular *sovereignty,* not just the popular *franchise,* Guizot placed himself and the conservative Orleanists among the broad grouping of European conservatives (Manent 1994, 100). When one thinks about French conservatism, it is important to distinguish between two different groups. One group included firmly conservative Legitimists—supporters of the Bourbons—who had long been more closely tied to the reactionary elements in the church hierarchy. The other group included the Orleanists—supporters of the junior branch of the royal line—who were initially more moderate in their attitude toward the church. Once in the government of the July Monarchy, however, the Orleanists seized the opportunity to increase their own power within a restricted electorate by appealing to the church and its supporters.

The emerging conservative Orleanists, led by François Guizot, saw an opportunity to increase their own power by appealing to the church and its supporters. The government promised to grant the church more authority and more state resources. Guizot and his supporters made state-church relations a central topic of debate in parliament. Opponents of Guizot, such as Adolphe Thiers and Victor Cousin in the chamber, or Jules Michelet and Edgar Quinet in the Collège de France, were equally quick to use anticlericalism in the attempt to unseat the government (Furet 1992, 351ff). As early as 1833 Guizot proposed an educational law that would have given priests *ex officio* seats on local boards of education, and in 1838 he called upon Catholics to support a government that maintained social order (Johnson 1963, 206). In the 1840s Guizot's government adopted proclerical measures in education, foreign, and dynastic policy. Guizot proposed to curtail the state's monopoly on the certification of teachers and recognize the rights of the Catholic Church to exercise authority in this area. In a speech to the assembly, Guizot declared that the rights of parents and of religious beliefs took precedence over those of the state (Dansette 1961 [1948], 1:240). In external relations, Guizot offered to join with Austrian reactionary Prince Metternich in protecting the Catholic cantons of Switzerland against Protestant liberals in Zurich, Geneva, and Bern. As for dynastic politics, Guizot's government supported the conservative Bourbon dynasties in Spain and Naples, among whom Louis Philippe sought marriage partners for his sons. Guizot was not as far to the right as many of his supporters, as can be seen in the long delays in enacting the new legislation on education; in this situation, Guizot tacked between his supporters on one side and Adolphe Thiers and the anticlerical opposition on the other.

The new emphasis on religious issues strengthened the conservative government's position against the opposition and increasingly came to define the highly variable political alignments of the July Monarchy. Conservative forces grew through the debate over education and as Montalembert mobilized the conservative Catholic electorate in favor of the government. With no other major topics of national debate to affect the elections, Guizot judged 1846 a propitious year to call an election. Guizot was proven correct when the elections produced a majority for the government of about 100 deputies, the largest government majority in the life of the constitutional monarchy. Among the government's supporters were 146 deputies endorsed by Montalembert who would in 1847 provide the necessary votes enabling conservatives to reject franchise reform (by 98 votes). As Louis Girard argues: "The July Monarchy remained without roots. To make up for this defect, it tried to unite itself with a party of social conservatives who feared the Jacobin and the revolutionary tradition" (1966, 121). The reintroduction of religious issues into ministerial politics helped to replace the ill-defined and variable parliamentary groupings of the 1830s with the more enduring division of the 1840s.

The republican movement was broad enough to provoke scholarly debate about how fully liberal was each aspect of the movement. Complex relationships between liberalism and republicanism—and between liberals and republicans—cannot be neatly summarized. Ronald Aminzade argues that French republicanism "can be understood in terms of a relatively fluid ideology and practice that combined the ability to integrate diverse, and sometimes, divergent, elements from various political traditions" that range from liberalism to socialism (1993, 262).

In part, the relationships between liberalism and republicanism changed over time. In the Revolution of 1830, liberals shared a commitment to strengthening parliamentary and constitutional government, protecting economic individualism, and limiting the authority of the Catholic Church in political institutions. Early liberals opposed authority for a church in political institutions, and the Revolution of 1830 was marked by violent anticlerical incidents. Still, many liberals did not necessarily oppose the church as an important institution in society. It is important to remember that a central tenet of classical liberalism, freedom of religion, did not mean the destruction of all religious institutions; for all their belief in individualism, many liberals continued to emphasize the importance of religion in maintaining social stability and order. As the 1830s wore on, and certainly by 1840, opposition to the Catholic Church grew out of fashion among some members of the political elite (Rémond 1969, 120). On the question of religion, some erstwhile liberals drifted to the right, while others, by remaining opposed to the Catholic Church, stayed closer to the republican movement.

One of the main distinctions between republicans and liberals was their attitude toward the monarchy: In the 1830s, republicans had looked more favorably upon the revolutionary tradition and had ties to revolutionaries such as Alexandre Ledru-Rollin. Liberals approved the revolution but were more concerned by its terrorist phase; they favored a constitutional monarchy to ensure the legality, if not the legitimacy, that could be provided by a king (Manent 1994, 80; Girard 1966, 120–22).

The final years of the July Monarchy saw rapprochement between republicans and left-leaning liberals, with both groups pushing for parliamentary and electoral reform. Alexis de Tocqueville argued that the refusal to extend citizenship rights more broadly helped provoke the Revolution of 1848 and bring to an end France's great liberal experiment (1970, 1–58). Progressives offered several franchise reform proposals that failed in the chamber during the 1840s and their final strategy—to mobilize mass support in the form of public banquets—unwittingly became the occasion for the public riots in February that quickly brought down the regime. Ironically, the resistance to reform deprived the government of the option to respond with force, since the government's main armed support came from the National Guard and the middle-class men it comprised. These men were socially conservative but excluded from the franchise by the high tax requirement. According to Tocqueville, an enfranchised National Guard could have protected a government against urban riots in early February or the National Guard could have imposed a liberal regency after Louis Philippe's late February abdication. If the reforms had been made in time, and at least a modest fraction of the middle classes enfranchised, the constitutional monarchy could have continued through 1848.

This explicitly counterfactual argument of Tocqueville's should not be taken too far. Nondemocratic governments often survive with the implicit support of middle-class groups that are formally excluded from participation, although it may be true that long-term survival can be made more difficult by formal exclusion. Tocqueville's argument assumes that progressive regimes are more stable than conservative ones, at least in some circumstances. Other conservative regimes in France and elsewhere in Europe, albeit after 1848, engineered suffrage extensions that did not undermine their power. Whatever one makes of these possibilities in France before 1848, key problems for the survival of the regime lay in the opportunities to become more democratic that were missed. As Gordon Wright observes, "It is tempting to conclude that no other regime in modern French history missed so good an opportunity to perpetuate itself as a durable system" (1987 [1960]).

The failure of the constitutional monarchy either to survive on its own terms or to develop more democratic institutions illustrates the consequences of an influential, antiliberal clergy aligned with conservative political leaders. Liberals had few viable options open to them. Tocqueville, for example, could not bring himself to support any major political force, whether the Catholic revival's mingling of politics and religion or the progressives' threat to property (Jardin 1988, 343–69, 382–403). Experiencing what he saw as the incompatibility of these modern social movements and a regime of liberty, he offers more pessimistic views about the prospects for liberty than many contemporary analysts.[8] Despite their different evaluations of the possibilities for liberal democracy, Tocqueville and contemporary analysts identify similar potential threats: stalemate among democratic institutions (Mainwaring and Shugart 1993; Linz and Valenzuela 1994), economic crises (Przeworski, Alvarez,

---

8. See the qualified optimism in Remmer 1995, 103–22; Przeworski, Alvarez, Cheibub, and Limongi 1996, 39–55; and Przeworski and Limongi 1997. Diamond classifies about 75 of the world's 191 countries as liberal democracies in 1995, but the title "Is the Third Wave of Democratization Over?" reflects concerns that the "bull market" in democratic transitions may have run its course (1996). For qualified pessimism see O'Donnell 1996.

Cheibub, and Limongi 1996), and anti-Enlightenment religious fundamentalism (Huntington 1996). In mid-nineteenth-century France, these factors combined to produce a virtually impossible situation for would-be supporters of liberal reform.

Anticlericalism and the Third Republic, 1870–1940

After the failure of the first liberal experiment during the constitutional monarchy, and as the Second Empire entered its second decade in the 1860s, French liberals increasingly came to support the idea of creating a republic. Thiers exemplifies the transformation of liberals from constitutional monarchists into republicans.[9] For all his antipathy to Guizot and Guizot's shift to the right, Thiers had been a committed supporter of the July Monarchy. Thiers' speech in 1864 as a member of the minority opposition in the assembly of the Second Empire is seen as a key moment in the emergence of liberals as republicans. Thiers and other "new" republicans served as the main opposition, both to Louis Napoleon under the Second Empire and then to conservatives during the first years of the as yet undefined successor regime.

A social movement organized during Louis Napoleon's empire and in the first few years of the Third Republic to produce "a counter-elite anchored in autonomous institutions and buoyed by an alternative political culture" (Nord 1995a, 38). This counterelite led a "resurrection of civil society" essential for the transition to a democratic regime (Nord 1995b, 9). In my view, the most important middle-class social movements organized around the theme of anticlericalism. Masonic lodges, Protestant lay organizations, and educational societies all opposed the Catholic Church. Unlike the Lamennaisian movement under the constitutional monarchy, these social movements were outside of the church. Also in contrast to the earlier movement, members of these organizations successfully challenged the church's authority in the political arena. They forged alliances with liberals, and their members often ran as Republican candidates. The most important educational society, Jean Macé's Ligue de l'Enseignement "gathered, sustained, and in some measure reconciled the nation's secular democrats . . . it helped these men to prevail" (Auspitz 1982, 165). By 1885, Jean Macé had been elected senator and one-third of the Chamber of Deputies were members of the league.

The survival of the Third Republic seemed to be a very open question in the 1870s, not the least because conservatives predominated in its early assemblies (Berstein and Berstein 1987). The first elections, held in February of

---

9. For a classification of Thiers consonant with this view, see Agulhon 1993, 24.

1871, centered on the issue of peace or continued war with Prussia and conservative local notables campaigning to end the war won the majority of seats. The assembly chose Thiers to lead the government during its first two years (1871–73), but conservatives forced him out when they could do without him. Many conservatives viewed the emerging republican institutions as a temporary expedient until conflicts between the pretenders and the intransigence of the senior pretender could be resolved, if by no other means than the natural death of the aged Comte de Chambord. The presidency of the conservative Count MacMahon (1873–79) was intended to be a brief holding regime, not the first episode in establishing a republic.

Electoral support for republicans grew in this critical decade. In the last elections under the Empire in 1869, republicans won in urban areas. By 1877 republicans won a broad national mandate (Nord 1995a, 45). Rueschemeyer, Stephens, and Stephens argue that the class coalition behind the republican movement now included, "politically active urban middle classes and the provincial bourgeoisie" (whereas, under the constitutional monarchy, it had included "politically active artisans and the urban middle classes") (1992, 90). In their account, the change in the political orientation of the provincial bourgeoisie in favor of the republican movement proved to be the decisive change in the class coalition. Their insight provides a jumping off point: if the changed political orientation of the provincial bourgeoisie is the key behind the success of the Third Republic, what explains that change? Why were liberals able to gain support in this period, but not before? What was the logic underlying the liberal coalition? In what ways did anticlericalism serve to mobilize support for republicans?

Support for republicans among members of the Ligue de l'Enseignement centered on the issue of anticlericalism and educational reform. Since the mid-1860s, members of the league had actively sought to destroy the church-controlled educational system and to create a unified national identity through a fully secular system of primary education. The league itself was born out of opposition to the Falloux law of 1850 which had given control over primary education to the clergy. Begun in the Alsace region which was predominantly Catholic, the league's first members were Protestants. During the 1870s under MacMahon's presidency, members of the league along with republicans had been targeted for harassment by prefects, police, and government informers (Auspitz 1982, 123–60). Thus, the natural affinity based on secularizing goals shared by the republicans and members of the league was solidified in the first years of the Third Republic through their common interest in defeating conservatives.

The movement was strongly influenced by the structure of political opportunity (Tarrow 1994, 85ff and 232, fn. 13). The political opening of the first direct election of a president under male suffrage in 1848 made possible a national republican organization with a central committee in Paris and a total of 353 branches in sixty-two of France's eighty-six departments (Aminzade 1993, 30–31). During the subsequent period of repression, under Louis Napoleon, the nascent republican movement had been organized into *chambrées* (village or drinking societies), educational societies, and other nonovertly political organizations. Beginning in the 1860s, republicans developed a culture of opposition to the empire mainly by organizing "in opposition to the power and privilege of the counterrevolutionary church—its exemption from laws restricting free association, its immunity from press censorship, [and] its decisive control over education and public assistance" (Auspitz 1982, 18). Once the repression ended in the 1870s, the republican movement was mobilized in explicitly political ways. Educational societies offered direct support to republican candidates and republicans also garnered support from other middle-class social organizations such as the Masonic lodges. As secret societies, the Masonic lodges had repeatedly come under attack from the church. By the 1870s Masonic lodges came to serve as a training ground for republican politicians, often providing key social networks for urban middle-class men with political ambitions.

If links between organized middle-class groups and republicans were forged by social movement organizations, understanding the support peasants gave to the Third Republic through less formally organized movements is more challenging. Yet rural social groups must be included in a full explanation of why republicans failed or succeeded. More than 70 percent of the population lived in small communities (those with less than 5,000 people) in 1877, while only 20 percent of the population lived in large communities (those with more than 10,000 people). Forty percent of the economically active population was counted in the agricultural sector in each census from 1881 through 1901.[10] Failing to gain rural support under a system of universal male suffrage would surely have defeated liberals in the Third Republic.

The 1876 election gave republicans a majority in the assembly and the question of whether France should return to a monarchy or preserve a republican form of government was put to the voters decisively in 1877. In the Crisis

---

10. Figures for 1877 interpolated from surrounding years in Flora and Alber 1987, 2:259, 494.

of May 16th, President MacMahon appointed a conservative government without support from a majority of deputies, dissolved the assembly, and called new elections. Anticlerical peasants decided overwhelmingly in favor of a republic. In other words, once the theme of war versus peace receded, anticlerical peasant support for conservative local notables evaporated. When issues centered on the question of regime type (monarchy versus republic), anticlerical peasants supported the party that opposed the authority of the church. Combined with middle-class social movements, these anticlerical peasants made possible an enduring republican majority in the assembly.

Anticlerical peasant support for republicans after 1877 was based on the growing political organization of the Republican party, rather than narrow economic interests. For example, anticlerical peasants continued to support republicans throughout the 1880s despite the increasing economic pressure faced by peasants. Throughout the 1880s republicans offered only mixed support for tariff protection and passed legislation that protected industry, not agriculture. Nevertheless, anticlerical peasants supported republicans against conservative, proclerical candidates that promised full tariff protection. Anticlericalism had historical roots in the countryside because of the church's relationship to land tenure and the rural economy. The church had been a more substantial landholder in France than in Belgium (Pounds 1990, 229). Belgian landholding differed in that feudal obligations under the old regime had declined even further than in France and the proportion of the land held by the clergy was smaller (Milward and Saul 1973, 47–53, 60). As a result, there was more animosity toward the church in France, more land that was expropriated and sold during the Revolution of 1789, and more widespread rural anticlericalism throughout the nineteenth century.

Perhaps the clearest illustration of the importance of political and religious interests over explicitly economic concerns was the Boulanger Affair of 1889. Elections in 1889 preceded the major tariff reform of 1892, yet "a surprising lack of public debate on economic matters" took place.[11] Instead, the main issue was again a constitutional question: should the Republic be continued or, should the government of France be placed in the hands of an antirepublican military officer, General Boulanger? Silence on the tariff question was evident in the Paris press, which offered "rare, minor notices regarding the question of protection," and in Méline's own major campaign address, which "contained only an incidental reference to tariffs." Efforts made by conservative protec-

---

11. Quotations and analysis in this paragraph from Golob 1944, 155–56, n. 37, 246.

tionists to organize peasants into agricultural syndicates failed, mainly because of the inability of socially conservative elites to attract a large following. Republicans maintained their dominance by focusing on anticlerical sentiment among the peasantry. Thus, although conservatives may have passed agricultural protection legislation sooner, anticlerical peasants were not willing to concede to conservatives on other issues such as increasing the role of the church in the state.

The argument that anticlericalism was a necessary precondition for peasants to support republicans is further shown when one compares regions in France. For if the intersection of anticlericalism and social classes accounts for patterns of political outcomes, then wherever peasants were proclerical they should not support republicans. France's department in the far northeast, the Nord, provides clear evidence: the church had relatively minor landholdings under the ancien régime and the Revolution of 1789 redistributed very little, so the peasants of the Nord were proclerical and antirepublican. Peasants in the Lys basin and the north of the department were hostile to the Republic because it threatened the interests of the church (although the industrial bourgeoisie in Lille and the southern half of the department rallied to the republican cause) (Ménager 1983, 1263). In contrast to France as a whole, which we have seen supported republicans in the elections of 1877 and during the 1880s, the Nord went to the monarchical right (Hilaire et al. 1977, 9). "An independent peasantry," writes Jean-Marie Mayeur (1984, 207), "attached to the Church and clergy, but hostile to the leadership of notables, took a chance on christian democracy, politically on the right, according to the criteria of the time, socially on the left." In the northern half of the department, the republicans' secularizing program for education produced an antiliberal backlash in the countryside. As Bernard Ménager reports,

> The religious convictions and the influence of the clergy remained intact and, in 1877, the left was the victim of the anticlericalism of its leaders. In 1881, the left took revenge thanks to a moderate Republican before ceding anew to the stronger in the school debate. In 1893, the victory of the abbé Lemire marked the alliance of the people and the clergy. (1983, 1219)

From the 1890s on, the Nord was a bastion of the new force of political Catholicism, leaving liberals to an increasingly narrow base among the urban middle classes in that department.

Republican predominance was also shaped by the strategy of the Catholic Church. French republicans repeatedly assaulted the church's role in education, with the most important reform coming in 1882 (Gildea 1983, 27). After 1860, Belgian liberals took increasingly important steps against the role of the clergy in public instruction, with the critical legislation coming in 1879. The Catholic Church in France counseled accommodation to the (comparatively harsh) French education law of 1882, while the Catholic Church in Belgium had advocated resistance to the (comparatively lenient) Belgian education law of 1879.[12] Liberal journals fondly cited French Catholic attempts to amend the proposed law of 1882 precisely along the lines already laid out in the Belgian law of 1879.[13] The Belgian Minister of Education and author of the 1879 law, Van Humbéeck, raised the same point in parliamentary debate.[14] The French Catholics' willingness to tolerate the Republican assault on clerical authority in education contrasted sharply with the confrontational response of Belgian Catholics.

The church had different resources and faced a different situation in France and Belgium. Stathis Kalyvas argues that the French church reasonably expected republican regimes to be short-lived and therefore relied on its alliance with antisystem political elites to avoid the costs of independent political organizing, while the Belgian church reasonably expected the basic outlines of the liberal regime to persist and therefore Belgian clergy were willing to engage in costly organizing (1996, 114ff, 141). Compounding this difference, the Belgian church's organizational response soon gave it greater resources with which to resist the liberal assault on clerical authority. In Belgium, the church was able to provide virtually every pupil the alternative of attending a parochial school. The church could therefore deal harshly with those who did not send their children to its schools. In France, however, many areas were already served only by state schools. The French church therefore had fewer options to offer its faithful. The recommendations of a church official in Paris indicated how the church expected the devout to respond: parents were to send their children to parochial schools if possible

> but you will not find Christian schools everywhere. If you have in your neighborhood only one school, and if in this one school religion is not

---

12. Belgian liberals paid close attention to developments in church-state relations in France. The office of Frère-Orban collected newspaper clippings from the liberal and Catholic press on matters of education in both Belgium and France. The file of collected clippings, with annotations, is now located in the Fonds Frère-Orban, Archives Générales du Royaume de Belgique.

13. Article 4 of the Belgian law of 1879 figured prominently here: it provided for religious instruction in public schools by the clergy outside of regular school hours. Even this compromise position was rejected in the final form of the French legislation.

14. *Le Précuseur* (Brussels, March 30, 1882).

taught, you have a double duty to fulfill. First, you must see to the Christian instruction of your children yourselves; this obligation, of which nothing may relieve you, becomes more pressing than ever before, when you can no longer delegate it to the teacher. . . . In the second place, you must assure yourself, through a vigilant watch, that the faith of your children is exposed to no peril in the school which they frequent. . . . The dangers which we bring to your attention here could only be present as abuses; but abuse is possible, and it is up to fathers and mothers to be attentive and uncover abuse if it presents itself.[15]

The response of the French church to the laicization of education was moderated by the absence of an alternative educational system. The contrast between how the church in France and Belgium would respond was evident to liberals at the time. Gambetta, leader of the left wing of the opportunist radicals in France made the phrase, "Le cléricalisme, voilà l'ennemi," a rallying cry. Janson, the Belgian progressive who had long identified with Gambetta, responded: "Ceux qui nous convient à nous grouper, au cri du guerre de Gambetta: 'Le cléricalisme, voilà l'ennemi,' dans le même instant, introduisent l'ennemi dans la place" (Delange-Janson 1962, 1:346).

By the end of the 1870s the two great traditions of liberalism and republicanism had shed most of their differences regarding questions of regime. In part, this was due to the influence of liberal institutions themselves.

In 1875, a constitution liberal in its essence because of its balance of powers and its concern to restrain the propensities of universal suffrage was bequeathed to French Republicanism that until then had very different traditions. Republicanism accommodated itself to the constitution and the Republican powers would inhabit the constitution with a few minor changes until the Second World War. (Jardin 1985, 416, my translation)

The Third Republic rested on the fundamental liberal principles of constitutionalism, parliamentarism, economic individualism, and the separation of religious and political institutions in a regime that lasted from the 1870s to 1940.

Republican and even Radical programs built on essential features of nineteenth-century liberalism. Liberals, Republicans, and Radicals diverged in their attention to social inequality, roughly in the order listed here. Even so, even the Radicals' policy proposals to ameliorate inequality were aimed to-

---

15. Pastoral letter, as cited in *L'Echo du Parlement* (Brussels, April 28, 1882).

ward the gradual evolution of society with varying degrees of state intervention that did not challenge the right to own property. Émile Auguste Chartier, writing virtually daily after 1906 under the name Alain in *La Dépêche de Rouen,* exercised considerable influence on Radical thought and has been said to incarnate Radical philosophy. His column, "Propos d'un Norman," emphasized such classic liberal themes as the search for happiness through liberty, self-reliance, anticlericalism, and state education (Berstein and Berstein 1987, 17). Republicans and Radicals shared the key liberal principles of constitutionalism, the desire to separate church and state, and respect for private property.

Conclusion

A new combination of liberal forces based in the anticlerical movement built a liberal regime that was more stable than any previous regime in France, including the constitutional monarchy. The anticlerical education societies and republican movement sought to reduce the entanglements of church and state, like the liberal Catholic movement of the 1820s and early 1830s; unlike their clerical leadership, however, anticlerical movements were led by secular elites. After coming to power in 1877, republicans adopted school reforms which effectively eliminated church control over primary public education and, in 1905, republicans passed formal legislation separating church and state. Support from urban middle classes and workers, as well as continued support from anticlerical peasants, succeeded in holding the liberal regime together throughout such challenges from the right as the Boulanger Affair in 1889.

As an important caveat to any consideration of the Third Republic, one must note that the "republican synthesis" was deeply flawed. The Dreyfus Affair roiled the political scene from 1894 on and this persecution of a Jewish officer (on false charges of espionage for the German army) reflected another attempt of the Catholic Church and the Army's High Command to exercise their institutional authority over citizenship and officeholding in the state. The synthesis was also flawed when it came to confronting the attractions of communism and fascism in the 1930s. In Stanley Hoffmann's memorable phrase, the "stalemate society" was remarkable more for its weak presidents, parliamentary intrigues, and modest legislative accomplishments in the interwar period (1963, 1–117).[16] The late and partial consolidation of liberalism in France left it on shakier grounds than in countries where liberals had held or

---

16. Echoes of Hoffmann's negative evaluation—and also dissenting voices of praise—may be heard in Horvath-Peterson 1991, 302–3.

shared power from 1830 on, as in Belgium, Britain, the Netherlands, and Switzerland. Like regimes in these aforementioned countries, the French Third Republic withstood the economic crisis of 1873–96, World War I, and the Great Depression. Unlike these other regimes, the Third Republic did not survive World War II. The Vichy regime was considerably more than a German imposition, for it returned to power the military and socially conservative, proclerical political groups (Paxton 1982 [1972]), precisely those groups excluded by a republican coalition that included anticlerical peasants and urban middle classes.

Chapter 4

Failed Reform and Co-opted Defeat in Germany

Why have liberal parties in Germany been weak? The signs of weakness were hard to dispute. Conservative monarchs prevailed when liberals pushed for constitutionalism and parliamentary governance in the German states in the Revolutions of 1830 and 1848 and in the constitutional crises of the 1860s. With Prussian military successes in 1866 over Austria and in 1870 over France the likelihood of liberal political reforms declined; the liberal movement split into a progovernment wing, the National Liberals, and a proreform wing, the Progressives. In the late 1860s and in the newly unified Germany in the 1870s, National Liberals served as junior partners in authoritarian governments. In the 1890s and early twentieth century, parliamentary politics acquired greater significance, but fully constitutional government continued to elude Germany until after World War I (Blackbourn 1984, 192, 278). Germany had a liberal movement that was strong enough "to challenge for power and even to put its imprint on German political development but that was too weak to bring German politics under its permanent control" (Jarausch and Jones 1990, 23).

The question of German liberalism is important because of liberalism's many consequences. The patterns of nineteenth-century politics bequeathed to the new Weimar Republic in 1919 little constitutional experience with which to manage the economic and social crises of the 1930s. At the level of mass politics, the weakness of liberal organizations and the prior connections to authoritarian elites left many former supporters of liberal parties susceptible to appeals for new forms of authoritarianism (Childers 1983). In the post–World War II era, Christian Democrats and Socialists set the political agenda and supported a political economy that was more corporatist than that of Switzerland or France, where liberals had exercised greater power in the nineteenth and early twentieth centuries (Katzenstein 1984, 1985).

In addition, a study of liberalism must include examples of failed attempts to build liberal regimes, as can be found in the German experience, for the comparative method is at its best when diverse outcomes comprise a single analysis. This means that the problems of studying German liberalism must be confronted directly. One must carefully distinguish between the middle classes and liberalism. The difference between a social class and a political movement should be obvious, but in the case of Germany, the extended arguments of David Blackbourn and Geoff Eley have reminded scholars that the middle classes are not necessarily liberal in their political orientation. There were many ways in which the middle classes exercised their influence in German society other than through liberal parties and there were many other factors besides the strength of the middle class that influenced liberal parties. One must also distinguish between the various goals of liberals and recognize that particular political arrangements could satisfy some but not all of them. In doing so, it is not sufficient to argue that German liberals' acceptance of some partial victories explains their failure to obtain a full victory; the reasons why a full victory were not possible must be explored.

I shall focus on the organizational ties between churches, states, and social classes as the key facts. As Dietrich Rueschemeyer, Evelyne Huber Stephens, and John Stephens put it, "it is the social organization of religion and its relation to classes and the state rather than its doctrinal content that was pivotal, though there is some relation between the two" (1992, 275). I shall argue that we can build on the institutional approach by specifying the mechanisms by which states exerted influence over religious administration. State control of churches in the early nineteenth century allowed the leaders of Protestant states to use conservative movements within the churches to oppose political reform. Social and religious movements that elsewhere provided organizational bases for liberalism were turned to the advantage of conservative elites or were severely weakened. This chapter aims to understand the dynamic process by which states exerted control within and through churches, and thereby identify the conditions under which religious institutions can be used by conservative state elites. It also seeks to specify, by examining the role of the Catholic Church in Germany, the conditions under which religious institutions increasingly separate from the state chose to support or oppose liberalism.

Religion as a Cultural Resource of German Liberalism, 1815–48

The German liberal movement drew upon religion as a cultural resource, that is, liberal leaders highlighted ideas, beliefs, and attitudes drawn from their religious background that seemed conducive to the liberal movement. Liberal

TABLE 5. Institutions, Reform Dynamics, and Outcomes in Germany

Elite Phase

State and Church Institutions at Onset of Liberal Reform	*Non-liberal, incorporated churches* Neo-absolutist monarchies, established Protestant churches, allied Catholic Church; Prussia and Austria-Hungary leading powers in 1815	
Liberal Policy toward Religious Authority	*Attack* Foster Protestant dissent	*Attack* Support breakaway Catholic Church
Response of Clergy	*Opposition* Accept Pietist, direction, support monarchs	*Opposition* Ally with monarchs
Fate of Elite Liberal Reform	**Failed** No effective constitutions in major states despite reform attempts in 1840s	

Mass Phase

Institutions at Onset of Second Liberal Reform	*Monarchs sovereign* Established Protestant churches and more autonomous Catholic church	
Liberal Policy toward Religious Authority	*Preserve* Retain Protestant churches	*Attack* Curtail Catholic Church authority
Response of Clergy	*Toleration* Prussia's Protestant clergy aid conservative parties	*Opposition* Catholic clergy aid prochurch party
Provincial Middle-Class and Peasant Reply	*Tolerate liberals* Prussian Protestants support conservative parties	*Oppose liberals* Catholics accept mobilization by Catholic party
Party and Regime Outcome	**Co-opted Defeat of Liberals** *Weak liberal parties in an authoritarian regime* Liberals support national, economic, religious policies, but do not secure constitutional controls on executive power	

organizers evoked common religious sentiments, espoused shared religious ideals, and deployed religious symbolism to mobilize and motivate their supporters. When religion was used as a cultural resource in this way, the connections between liberalism and religion existed mainly at the level of rhetoric. This is not to say that the rhetoric had no effect, as appeals on this basis could be quite effective in an era of limited electoral organizations. One crucial limitation of these rhetorical connections was that they were drawn upon only by liberal elites: religious organizations and clergy did not use their religious authority to help build support for liberalism. In this chapter we shall see how a few clergy with liberal sympathies sought to turn religious organizations into organizational supporters of liberalism, but also how these efforts did not meet with success. In drawing upon religion as a cultural resource, German liberals developed a political movement that was virtually without support from pre-existing religious institutions.

A second crucial limitation of the rhetorical connections was that liberal organizers drew upon religion unequally, with favoritism to Protestantism over Catholicism expressed quite clearly. Without an attempt to bridge Protestantism and Catholicism, any political movement could be limited. Protestants comprised about 45 percent of the Christian population in the states of the German Confederation, and were predominant in northern, eastern, and central states. One of Germany's two great powers, Prussia, had a population that was 65 percent Protestant while the other, Austria, had a population that was more than 95 percent Catholic. Catholics comprised about 55 percent of the Christian population of the member states of the German Confederation, including German Austria. Predominantly Catholic regions ran south from western Hannover, through the Rhineland and down to Baden, then east to Bavaria and Austria; a second concentration of Catholics lived in a band from Danzig south to Breslau and Silesia. Conservative clerical organizing within the Catholic Church, as we shall see in this chapter, produced more effective political action than any effort of the liberal movement.

If German liberals used religion mainly as a cultural resource, it was not for lack of trying other ways of drawing upon religion to promote liberalism. They attempted to draw upon the organizational bases provided by religious institutions and also to build movements of countermobilization against churches, but neither effort met with success. These organizing efforts took place in the 1830s and 1840s and their failure, by and large, helped produce the liberal defeat in the Revolution of 1848. Given the differences between Protestantism and Catholicism and the organizational focus of this analysis, it makes sense to consider each confession separately.

Protestantism

Liberals drew mainly upon Protestantism as a cultural resource. The following examples could easily be multiplied: a key liberal group, the national student movement, held its first mass demonstration to celebrate a Protestant milestone, the third centenary of Martin Luther's 95 Theses. Prominent liberal leader Jacob Siebenpfeiffer called for a "political Luther" to save the nation when he spoke at the liberals' most important mass gathering, the Hambacher Fest of 1832. Siebenpfeiffer, like many liberals, further claimed that Protestantism provided a prerequisite for the emancipation of the citizen, religious freedom (Langewiesche 1988a, 35; Thadden 1983, 96). Moderate liberal Rudolf Haym similarly interpreted the renaissance, Protestant Reformation, Enlightenment, idealism, and liberalism as a continuous historical development (Rosenberg 1933, 85ff). Although there were exceptions, most of Germany's leading liberals in the early nineteenth century were from Protestant families and believed that their Protestantism naturally reinforced their liberal political views.

Liberals originally expected Protestant clergy to support them. Many clergy in 1815 held rationalist, or Enlightenment, theological views that were easily compatible with the liberal emphases on status equality and individualism. "A rational and just society," according to the prevalent view, "should be based on achievement and merit, and denied the innate superiority of any classes or persons" (Bigler 1972, 50). Even at the highest levels, the ideas of leading church administrators fit with a liberal accomodation of religious differences. Religious affairs in the Prussian state before 1840 were dominated by Baron Karl von Altenstein, for example, who as Minister of Ecclesiastical Affairs and Education sought unity within the Prussian state church by tolerating differing tendencies within it. Altenstein himself favored the right Hegelian approach, yet he opposed the appointment of extremist conservatives, such as Otto von Gerlach, and stalled the drive to force a liberal theologian, Friedrich Schleiermacher, from office.

Yet a conservative movement transformed Prussia's Protestant clerics into effective opponents of all forms of liberalism. The conservatives' leading organizer, Ernst Wilhelm Hengstenberg, determined "to make religion an instrument of reaction," to purge the church of the influences of rationalism, and to root out all possible forms of opposition to the will of the king. At least four journals that had previously been dedicated to religious issues now "bent every effort to convince the evangelical clergy that the political turmoil was essentially over religion. . . . [and] to abandon their own rivalries and support the conservative cause" (Shanahan 1954, 80, 201). Hengstenberg, as a professor and widely read journalist, came to dominate the formation of religious policy and changed the spirit of tolerance within the Prussian church. The appointment of Hengstenberg's sympathizer, Johann Albrecht Friedrich Eichhorn, as minister of Ecclesiastical Affairs and Education in 1840 marked the transition from Altenstein's latitudinarian toleration: Eichhorn announced that the government would no longer remain neutral in theological controversies and that the government "definitely favored those clergymen who identified themselves with its struggle against the political opposition." By the early 1840s, the movement had achieved a key goal: "rationalism and Hegelianism in the theological faculties no longer presented serious threats to the Hengstenberg faction's dominant influence over the clergy" (Bigler 1972, 118–19).

Once the conservative elite movement took control of the Protestant church, the church was quick to turn the advantage to their conservative political leaders. The absence of a separate clerical order or, in some states, the clergy's clear submission in a system of aristocratic patronage, and the fact that Protestant kings and princes served as the highest bishop in their territories, all offered vast administrative power over churches to the territorial ruler (Krieger 1972 [1957], 11; Kocka 1993, 28). Church officials used the administrative power to discipline lower clergy who threatened the new conservative spirit. For example, the rationalist Pastor F. W. Sintenis was out of step with the new conservatives. He condemned as idolatrous the public exhibition of a picture of Jesus and an accompanying verse commending the picture as a source of inspiration for intercessory prayer. According to pastors like Sintenis, Hengstenberg and his followers were *Finsterlinge* (Sons of Darkness), or *Dunkelmänner* (Men of Darkness). Sintenis was quickly censured for his views. In sum, the pietist movement purged the state church of rationalist influence and made it into a unified force against liberalism in the 1830s and 1840s.

Not all pastors and theologians accommodated themselves easily to the new conservative ascendancy. The most active opponents of conservatism banded together and acquired a name, *Lichtfreunde* (Friends of Light), that simultaneously indicated their opposition to the conservatives and their attachment to Enlightenment rationalism so dear to liberals. As Jacques Droz has observed, "the *Lichtfreunde* communities became the rallying point for all— rationalists, young Hegelians . . . —who fought against intellectual compulsion" (1966, 140).

These rationalist clerics organized an opposition to the new conservatism. Pastor Leberecht Uhlich called a meeting of sixteen colleagues to form a society of friends that would together "defend the achievements of the Enlightenment—tolerance and the moral freedom to criticize dogma—against the onslaught of church orthodoxy" (Holden 1954, 132n. 72). The immediate impetus for the formation of the movement was to protest the disciplining of their rationalist colleague mentioned above, Sintenis. Uhlich also advocated a renewal of the church from within through the more active participation of the laity. "Uhlich seemed to believe that, except for the Hengstenberg faction, most Protestants in the German states would join the Friends of Light in their struggle for intellectual freedom and for an independent *Volkskirche*" (Bigler 1972, 212).

The Friends of Light movement did grow beyond its small, clerical core. Perhaps 25,000 people, of whom most were lay, attended one or more meetings in the 1840s. Three months after the first meeting of the sixteen pastors, a second meeting included a "substantial number of men, for the most part members of the clergy" but also including, as Uhlich enthusiastically reported, "philologists, physicians, merchants, and publishers" (Holden 1954, 63). Attendance continued to grow at what were now semiannual conventions: in May 1842, more than 200 people, in September 1842, 150 people, and at Whitsuntide 1843, over 300. In September 1843, approximately 400 people attended, two-thirds of whom were laity, of whom about a fifth were teachers. Six hundred people attended the Whitsuntide 1844 meeting, and 800 the September 1844 meeting. At Whitsuntide 1845, two to three thousand people attended the meeting. Subscriptions to the newsletter of the movement grew from 2,100 in 1842 to more than 5,000 in the spring of 1843.

Yet the Friends of Light remained regionally and socially circumscribed. Branch societies were established mainly in northern Germany, in about 21 localities by 1845. The branch society in Magdeburg, although one of the largest, had a typical social composition; its first meeting in November 1841 was attended by 150 people "from the most esteemed and cultivated of the official and business classes," according to Uhlich. A petition protesting the disciplining of a pastor in 1845 garnered 4,903 signatures by circulating through Breslau and 52 neighboring cities and towns. More than 90 percent of the signers described themselves as state officials, workers in various industries, educators, or other urban professionals, while fewer than 10 percent (480) of the signers described themselves as landowners or *Rittergutsbesitzern* (Holden 1954, 93–94).

The Prusssian state church absorbed into its own structure the conservative religious movement, Pietism, and thereby reinforced conservative political and social forces. German Pietism, much like religious movements elsewhere in northern Europe and Britain, called for religious revival and renewed spirituality, but in Germany it was a movement based in the countryside that quickly became linked to aristrocratic and state patronage (Fulbrook 1983). Unlike some dissenting movements elsewhere, Pietism did not link up with the defense Enlightenment values such as individualism. Nor did Pietism lead to the formation of a separate religious organization, but was instead incorporated into the existing state church as an ideological justification. There were other long-standing traditions that reinforced the conservatism of the Prussian church establishment: the Reformation of 1519 strengthened the idea that the secular and religious authorities should be linked. This was not Luther's intention, but the result of his seeking protection of German princes from the hostile Catholic Church. The division of the German peoples into two faiths, conjoined with the often intense anti-Catholicism of the Protestant community, weakened dissent in Protestantism. Protestants in Prussia were divided into Calvinist and Lutheran branches, but these divisions merely emphasized the need of Prussian rulers to practice policies of religious toleration on doctrinal matters. Toleration prevented doctrine from becoming a matter of theological dispute with political implications; the only opposition to the union of the Lutheran and Calvinist churches occurred in non-Prussian lands that had small Catholic populations.

To sum up, by 1848 the liberals had at most 25,000 religiously mobilized sympathizers, almost exclusively in urban areas. Perhaps a few dozen Protestant clerics took part in the movement.[1] Meanwhile, the Protestant right had captured an organization with broader appeal. Almost all of the 6,000 Protestant clergy in Prussia accepted the conservative direction. The political implications of this situation can already be seen in outline form: liberals claimed Protestantism as their cultural heritage but had virtually no claim on Protestant institutions. We shall examine these political implications further, after we first consider developments in the Catholic Church.

Catholicism

A new conservative movement within the Catholic Church also provoked a social movement linked to political liberalism. Ultramontanism was this new conservative movement, and it should be seen not simply as a continuation of age-old tradition, but as a modern conservative phenomenon (Blackbourn

---

1. An exact figure does not appear in the literature; my estimate is based on Bigler 1972, 187–230 and Holden 1954. The figure for the total Protestant clergy is provided by Bigler 1972, x.

1991b, 779ff). Ultramontanism became an important stream in the German Church in the 1830s and 1840s and gained strength under Pope Pius IX (1846–78). The orientation to Rome was novel in that, by the end of the eighteenth century, most national Catholic hierarchies were effectively controlled by territorial rulers rather than the pope. Ultramontanism's modernity can be seen also in its relationship with institutional secularization: reduced state control of ecclesiastical matters gave Rome more authority over the various national hierarchies, and the more centralized hierarchy could assert its autonomy vis-à-vis states. Ultramontanism was new also in its use of modern means of communication and organizing, as we shall see below. Ultramontanist Catholicism opposed liberal individualism as well as class-based organization; it offered instead a corporate, cross-class, Christian solidarity.

One great accomplishment of ultramontanism was the harnessing of mass religiosity on behalf of the church's political interests. An important example of how popular religiosity became tied to the church's exercise of political power can be seen in the evolution of pilgrimages, as analyzed by Wolfgang Schieder (1979 [1974]).[2] In the eighteenth century, pilgrimages did not play a major role in the political planning of the Catholic Church. Pilgrimages were predominantly local, that is, they were focussed on local manifestations of religious magic. In organizational terms, they were typically presided over by local Catholic lay brotherhoods. Theological rationalists among the clergy typically opposed pilgrimages on the grounds that they encouraged inappropriate beliefs, such as quasipaganism and naturalism. Even nonrationalist clergy criticized pilgrimages for the opportunities they provided for unmonitored, licentious behavior, especially as pilgrimages took place outside of church.

Pilgrimages changed in the early nineteenth century, according to Schieder. They became translocal in character, as pilgrims travelled long distances for several days at a time. Pilgrimage organization acquired a new form, with responsibility taken from local lay associations and now assumed by the church itself. Even within the church organization there were changes as diocesan authorities took on greater responsibilities. Massive publicity campaigns and planning characterized the organizing efforts. One should not exaggerate the distinction between traditional and modern pilgrimages; nevertheless, one can still see the truth in the description of the new German pilgrimages as "pilgrimages from above."

---

2. Margaret Anderson (1995) criticizes Schieder for relying too heavily on a causal model in which all things happened at the behest of the clergy, but it remains clear that the outcome benefitted Catholic clergy in their complex relationship with the state.

The pilgrimages occurred where state and religious authorities were most at odds. The three most important pilgrimages—to Trier, Kevelaer, and the septennial display at Aachen—took place in the Rhineland, a confessionally mixed area ruled by a Protestant monarch, rather than in more strongly Catholic areas such as Bavaria or Austria. The pilgrims themselves came overwhelmingly from the Rhineland: 78 percent of the pilgrims to the Holy Coat at Trier lived in the diocese of Trier, and most of the rest came from elsewhere in the Rhineland. Five hundred thousand pilgrims saw the relic at Trier during seven weeks in the fall of 1844, making this pilgrimage the largest of all similar organized religious displays of the first half of the nineteenth century in Germany (calculated from Schieder 1979 [1974], 68). Drawing so many people pilgrimages helped to demonstrate the Catholic Church's ability to mobilize a mass following.

A countermovement against the new ultramontane conservatism developed within the Catholic Church and forged links with leading liberals. An excommunicated priest, Johannes Ronge, denounced the exhibition of the Holy Coat at Trier in a letter to the local bishop in October of 1844. Ronge called for the formation of a new and independent church free of papal control, a so-called German-Catholic church. Ronge and the German-Catholics applied rationalist and Enlightenment principles to oppose celibacy, the Latin Mass, auricular confession, and other elements of traditional Catholicism. German patriotism provided a constant subtheme of German-Catholic organizing. The German-Catholic movement advocated a subordination of the German-Catholic church to a newly unified and liberal German state. The movement was fully liberal in terms of lay congregational control and its strong ties to liberal leaders.

The German-Catholic movement did not incorporate powerful clerics. We have seen that the founder was a former priest at odds with Rome and the ultramontanism of the upper German hierarchy. Other leaders, like those of many German-Catholic congregations, were lay local elites. The predominance of lay leaders can be seen in the council in Leipzig that was called by the new congregations to develop a common constitution for the movement: "The deputies were largely members of the professional class, middle-class tradespeople, and representatives of the Roman Catholic priesthood who had renounced their vows" (Holden 1954, 140). Along with its middle-class leadership, the movement sought to develop more participatory and democratic governance of religious institutions. The deputies agreed without debate on a presbyterian organizational form and congregational rule; future meetings were to consist of congregational representatives, the council decided, of whom no more than one-third could be priests.

The German-Catholic movement achieved it greatest results, as Catherine Holden writes, "[i]n regions where Catholics constituted the minority in a mixed population or where the Roman Catholic church failed to receive the support of the secular authorities" (1954, 383). Although most of the early congregations were from Saxony, as was the elected president of the council, Prof. Wigard of Dresden, eventually more than half of the congregations were located in Prussia. The Breslau congregation in Prussia was always the largest, some 1,000 people signed a membership declaration during the congregation's founding in January and February of 1845 and over eight thousand belonged by 1847. Breslau offered favorable circumstances as Prussia's second largest city (after Berlin) and as the center of Silesian learning, industry, and government. In addition, the hostility of the Prussian government to Roman Catholicism had undermined the official church hierarchy, giving a dissenting movement a greater chance to break away. Silesia was also an ethnically and denominationally mixed province, both of which were favorable to a dissenting movement. By contrast, there were still only seven German-Catholic congregations in Catholic Baden by 1847, even though the movement enjoyed the sympathy of many Badenese liberals who sought to use the movement as an opportunity to reopen political questions.

Political Implications of Religious Opposition

Religious opposition groups during the 1840s helped the liberal movement acquire broader support. Liberal attitudes towards religious opposition focussed on just that fact: Arnold Ruge "welcomed the dissenting movements . . . as a means by which one of the major deficiencies of German liberalism, the lack of communication between its leadership and the masses, could be remedied." Gustav von Struve wrote that "German-Catholicism had managed to accomplish more in a matter of months than political liberalism had accomplished since the Wars of Liberation." Gervinus admired the "'almost instinctive cooperation of the great masses' which German-Catholicism had earned" (Holden 1954, 178–80). The liberal movement in the 1840s, Krieger writes,

> underwent an expansion to include for the first time organizations with intellectual leadership, a mass base, and a more than local scope. From

around 1844 both the German-Catholic sects and the free church movement of the Protestant Friends of Light began to find adherents numbering in the thousands among the burgher and more particularly petty burgher groups and to develop a consciousness of the liberal political implications in their clerical dissent. (1957, 284)

The 70,000 members of the German-Catholic church constituted perhaps the third largest single organization in the liberal movement overall.[3]

Yet the institutions of religious opposition were exceptionally weak organizations. Taking age as one proxy for organizational strength, the two dissent movements in Germany were each less than ten years old when the Revolution of 1848 occurred. Taking size as a proxy for strength, religious dissent encompassed vanishingly small fractions of the population: just 95,000 participants in Protestant dissent and German-Catholicism in all of Germany hardly compares to the populations of the states where these religious groups were most active—15.5 million people in Prussia and 1.8 million people in Saxony (population figures from Flora 1983b, 34). As for material resources, neither movement controlled property fully separate from the established Protestant church. Most congregations of the Friends of Light ceased their meetings when they were banned in 1845 and only a few movement radicals then separated from the church to form free religious communities; German-Catholics left their parent church, but then they depended on the established Protestant churches for places to worship. In sum, the movements of religious dissent in the 1840s offered German liberals remarkably little.

The churches remained dominant even as they adopted new tactics. The Protestant right, "[r]eligiously determined by the circle of Pomeranian pietists," and the Catholic collective movement both demonstrated their ability to attract a mass following in 1848 (Stadelman 1975 [1948], 97). Conservative Protestant clerics addressed the public directly. Pastors preached against revolution in local pulpits, organized local conservative societies, and helped support three inexpensive conservative journals aimed at a mass public. Conservative clerical organizing paid off with a set of "grass roots advocates more numerous and more zealous than those serving the other parties" (Shanahan 1954, 202). The ultramontanist movement within the Catholic Church created

---

3. Two other sets of organizations, both quasi-political recreational and cultural organizations, within the broad liberal movement were larger: membership in athletic societies is estimated around 85,000 and membership of the choral societies is estimated to have been at least 100,000 (Langewiesche 1988a, 37). A fourth set of organizations, student unions, also formed a training ground for future liberal and national leaders.

the largest mass movement in the German states before the Revolution of 1848. The organized public display of sacred relics attracted more visitors than any other public events in the years before the Revolution of 1848. Whereas just 25,000 people attended the most important gathering of the liberal movement, the Hambacher Fest of 1832, 500,000 people made the pilgrimage to Trier.

Key failures to reform neoabsolutist politics in German states in the 1830s and 1840s stemmed from the liberals' inability to employ religious issues in search for adequate allies. Liberals had virtually no preexisting movement of Protestant dissent on which to draw. Instead, they fostered new forms of dissent from the established Protestant churches with, as we have seen, relatively little success. The encouragement that liberals offered to the splinter German-Catholic movement underscored how the Catholic Church stood to lose authority in virtually any national, liberal regime. Further, the church's political supporters did not make common cause with predominantly Protestant liberals in the Frankfurt Parliament of 1848–49 when the opportunity for concerted action was arguably at its height, especially in the early months of the constitutional debate. Discussion of church-state issues in the parliament yielded little agreement, unclear compromises, and virtually no forward movement until the departure of many Austrian and Catholic delegates reinforced a rump majority by default. Liberals in 1848 also saw their weakness in relatively modest links to popular political sentiment as the era of elite politics came to a close. Many liberal leaders mistrusted the people whom they claimed to represent, and the cause lay not solely in Germany's underdeveloped technologies of mass communication nor only in the emergence of the social question, but also in the absence of durable, religiously based organizational ties between liberal elites and their possible constituents.

The legacy of liberal failures to capture the established church was an enduring limit to the liberal ability to draw upon Protestantism. Liberals could only draw on Protestantism as a cultural resource and could only claim to speak on behalf of Protestantism, while the vast preponderance of clerical leaders did not reciprocate. Instead, the vast resources of the established church were turned against the liberal movement, both within the church and in politics. The legacy of liberal failures to develop organizational links with the Catholic Church was a cycle of liberal and Catholic hostility. The few German-Catholics paled in comparison to the vast majority of loyal Catholics; in addition, Catholic leaders—not without reason—saw the liberal encouragement and support offered to the break-away faction as a direct attack on the church. The struggle between German liberals and Catholics was reinforced in many events and, as we shall see below, the successes of the Catholic Church in encouraging mass religious revival and the ability of political organizers to build a religious party limited liberal enthusiasm for mass participation in politics.

Liberals and Religious Politics, 1860–1914

German liberals suffered from their divorce from organized religion as the modern German state was constructed in the last half of the nineteenth century. The severity of the constraints imposed in Germany by the complex interaction of churches, states, and classes was, in Dieter Langewiesche's words, "unparalleled in the rest of Europe" (1990, 219). German liberals were largely deprived of the Catholic electorate, with only a few exceptions among Catholics who were urban, elite, anticlerical, and German nationalist. German liberals also had to compete with thoroughly Protestant conservative parties for the support of the Protestant peasants and middle classes. Not only did liberals compete with conservatives for support from these Protestant social groups, but they did so on entirely unequal terrain, as Protestant conservatives typically enjoyed the support of the established church. When the Socialist Party began its growth in the late 1880s, liberals had new competition for the secularized, Protestant working class.

Catholics supported self-identified liberals in the 1860s but not afterwards. A few statistics help to bear this out. For example, in the Prussian elections of the 1860s, Catholic districts (those with populations more than 55 percent Catholic) in Westphalia, Rhineland, and Hohenzollern elected liberal delegates three to one over clerical delegates. Deputies representing Catholic districts took liberal positions on key decisions in parliament: 66 percent of deputies from Catholic districts in the Rhineland and Westphalia followed liberals in rejecting the 1866 Indemnity Bill, whereas 55 percent of all Rhenish and Westphalian deputies rejected the bill and only 25 percent of all deputies did so. Catholic party mandates in the Prussian House of Representatives were less than 5 percent in 1866 (Anderson 1986, 84–88).

The 1870s and 1880s saw a surge in support for the Catholic Center party: In the Prussian House, Catholic mandates topped more than 20 percent of all seats with the election of 1873 and remained high thereafter. In the constituencies of the northern Rhineland and Westphalia with more than 40 percent of the electorate as Catholics, the turnout was 50 percent of registered voters and the Center party received 63 percent of the votes; by 1878 turnout had climbed to 68 percent and the Center party received 72 percent of the votes (Sperber 1984, 254). During the 1870s in the Ruhr, it is estimated that about 80 percent of

Catholic voters supported the Center in 1871 and 1874, a figure that climbed to over 90 percent in 1878 and peaked at close to 100 percent in 1881. In the Reich as a whole, just under half of the Catholic voters voted Center in 1871 while nearly three-quarters did so in 1881.[4]

These diverse statistics all show that modest Catholic support for liberal candidates and positions in the 1860s declined to near negligible levels in the 1870s and was replaced with solid Catholic support for Center party candidates. Given the Catholic and liberal cooperation in the 1860s, the military strength of the Prussian state in the 1860s cannot be eliminated from any full explanation for the failure to develop a liberal regime. Yet in the 1870s and thereafter, the deepening of the religious cleavage through popular religious revival and the formation of a political party on religious grounds contributed to the durability of the authoritarian regime and the continuing inability of liberals to win constitutional concessions.

Most of the new support for the Center party came from previously unmobilized new voters, rather than from former supporters of other parties. There were Catholics who continued to vote liberal, but these were relatively few, high social and economic status Catholics, mainly in urban areas with histories of Catholic anticlericalism, such as Cologne. Elite Catholics, who voted liberal, identified with the national and anticlerical mission of the liberal party, and the relatively higher social status of liberals compared to Catholic party organizers, rather than an alternative form of Catholic representation as such (Sperber 1984, 255–63).

In some instances, Catholicism offered opportunities to register dissent against the state and allied status and power elites. The victories of the Center party candidates in Silesia, for example, replaced deputies who were Catholic nobles with deputies who were equally Catholic, but decidedly commoners or lower clergy. "Universal suffrage, while not changing the structure of power or composition of elites," Margaret Anderson argues, "set in motion a revolution in social attitudes that shook the deference that had governed German social relations for centuries." Despite the best efforts of old elites to fit the new political forms—such as universal suffrage—into the old categories of previous experience, some enduring features of the traditional order permitted new voters to work their way towards political power. Religion was one of the most important elements of the old order to provide institutions, idioms, and opportunities for political opposition (Anderson 1993, 1451–55). Unfortu-

---

4. Rohe provides these figures and notes the caution with which they should be used (1986, 44n. 5, 119).

nately for German liberals, the means at hand for expressing grievances lead low-status Catholics not to support liberals, but instead to support clerical candidates.

The problem for liberals was not that they won support from the Protestant middle class, but that they, increasingly from 1860 to 1900, won support almost exclusively from the Protestant middle class. Liberals won support, as Stanley Suval writes, "in a modernized and industrialized environment that lies midway between the traditional rural agrarian areas and the cosmopolitanism of the big cities" (1985, 21). Suval concurs with James J. Sheehan's analysis:

> The typical liberal voter, therefore, was a Protestant who belonged somewhere in the middle range of the class and status hierarchies. . . . [Liberal districts] were composed of small and medium-sized towns, not great cities or distended industrial suburbs; when liberals did win large cities, it was most often in the relatively stable central districts where the urban middle strata still predominated. Similarly, their rural support came in places where agriculture was carried on by a large number of proprietors, not by a few big landowners. (1978, 246)

Liberals thus did best where they could rely on the survival of notable-style politics; they could not compete successfully against the new social mobilization of working classes in the largest cities or the more integrated social network of the Protestant church and landed-elite nexus in rural areas.

In general, the Protestant working class shared the individual-level secularization of the Protestant middle-class,[5] yet in the absence of organization, this shared outlook on religious authority was not sufficient to encourage Protestant workers to vote liberal. Whereas less than ten percent of votes in the heavily industrialized Ruhr region went to the Social Democratic Party (SPD) in the 1870s and 1880s, the party won nearly 20 percent of the votes by the end of the 1890s, and over 30 percent by 1912. In many of Germany's large cities, the SPD won only half as many votes as the liberal parties in the 1870s, but then won as many or more in the 1880s and 1890s (Rohe 1986, 116, 122). Not all of the SPD's votes came from workers, but the climb in SPD support indicates the growing mobilization of workers outside of the liberal parties. There were a few examples of conservative, religious, Pietist working-class

---

5. Individual-level secularization can be defined as the individual's unwillingness to submit her or his behavior to clerical authority, and it is often indicated by the failure to attend church, take communion, or marry a spouse from the same confession (Chaves 1994). Others define individual-level secularization as a matter of belief, yet employ the same behavioral markers as indicators. For a survey of religious behavior in Germany, see Smith 1995, 85–94.

groups strongly connected to the Protestant churches. These workers voted for conservative Protestant parties (as in Wuppertal and Bielefeld); only where more conservative candidates were not available, as in the Ruhr, did Pietist workers support National Liberal candidates (Rohe 1986, 26). In sum, secularized, nominally Protestant workers voted overwhelmingly for socialists, while Pietist workers supported conservative candidates or, when no alternative was available, National Liberal candidates. German liberals won neither the votes of the secular working class nor even the exclusive support of religiously mobilized workers.

The Kulturkampf and Liberalism

The relationship between German liberals and Catholicism was not determined by the desires of liberals alone; one cannot ignore the actions of the church. As Jonathan Steinberg suggests, the struggle between the Roman Church and European states played a role in the nineteenth century like that of the Cold War in the twentieth.[6] The pontificate of Pius IX (1846–78) was marked by his extreme antiliberalism. In the *Quanta Cura* and *Syllabus of Errors* in 1864, Pius IX condemned as errors such ideas as: "every man is free to embrace and profess that religion, which, guided by the light of reason, he holds to be true," "Protestantism is nothing else than a different form of the same true christian religion," and "the Roman Pontiff can and ought to reconcile and harmonize himself with progress, with liberalism, and with modern civilization."[7]

The major religious policy in the new Germany was the Kulturkampf, the state-led attack on the privileges of the Catholic Church. The government offered support to Catholic teachers in state schools who rejected Pius IX's 1870 dogma of papal infallibility, abolished the Catholic department in the Prussian ministry of religion in July of 1871, and dissolved the Jesuit order in June of 1872. The Falk Laws of 1873 placed the church under close state control and imposed government supervision over Catholic education, including education for the priesthood. In 1875, the government blocked the publication of a papal encyclical and passed laws to punish clergy who refused to abide by the earlier legislation; many bishops and priests went into exile rather than submit to the new order. Reconciliation with a new pope, Leo XIII, in 1878 and the repeal of the Falk Laws in the 1880s brought the Kulturkampf to

---

6. Personal communication, March 1996.
7. Pius IX, *Syllabus, Embracing the Principal Errors of Our Time* (1864), articles 15, 18, and 80.

an end. This Kulturkampf was "in many ways the most significant expression of liberalism's alliance with the Bismarckian state" (Sheehan 1978, 135).

One should not exaggerate the degree to which the church was hindered from carrying out its mission even at the height of the Kulturkampf, but many Catholic communities in Germany lost their priests; churches fell into disrepair and formerly clerical duties had to be assumed by the laity. The Kulturkampf caused secularization in the institutional authority of the church outside of ecclesiastical matters, as in the arts, theology, and education, and some secularization in the lay professionalization of selected internal organizational duties in the church (Anderson 1986).

The modest "successes" of the struggle against the Catholic Church in the realm of institutional secularization pale in comparison to the political failure. The Kulturkampf, as Blackbourn puts it, "left a political legacy that was the opposite of what liberals wanted. It made them beholden to Bismarck; and it helped to consolidate political Catholicism" (1987, 160). The political campaign against the Catholic Church changed political Catholicism in an unintended way. The Kulturkampf accelerated a preexisting trend of differentiation within the Catholic communities, namely, the differentiation of two roles: the political representation of the Catholic community in national politics and the exercise of clerical authority over religious matters. In Germany, as Anderson argues, the Kulturkampf accelerated the separation of the Center party from the hierarchy of the church itself (1995). Even as Center party candidates received the implicit and explicit aid of the church, the party made political calculations without direction from clergy. This, too, could be termed secularization—that is, the church lost direct control of its representation in national politics to the hands of professional, nonclerical party leaders. It was not the form of secularization that liberals or, for that matter, Bismarck, had intended.

Not only did the Center Party acquire an independent role in the representation of Catholic interests, but it also acquired a virtual monopoly on the political representation of Catholic interests. As Jonathan Sperber puts it, the Center party benefitted from the Kulturkampf because it "had established itself by 1871 as the unquestioned representative in the political arena of the Catholic milieu" (1984, 252). Although Anderson and Sperber disagree somewhat about the strength of the Catholic political subculture prior to 1870, with Sperber taking the position that great strides in political organization were taken in the 1850s and 1860s, both concur that the Kulturkampf strengthened the hold of the Center party on Catholic voters. Kalyvas forcefully argues that various attempts to form Catholic political parties had failed prior to 1866, and that the Prussian victory over Austria in that year, and the Kulturkampf in the united Germany, together deprived the church of support from a strong state in Germany and thereby provided the critical push for the successful development of the Catholic Center party (1996, 203ff).

Liberals enjoyed no comparable monopoly of Protestant political representation. When the Kulturkampf legislation was rescinded in the 1880s, one might have expected a backlash from Protestants' religiously motivated voting to aid the liberals, many of whom favored a continuation of the attacks on Catholicism, but this did not take place. Instead, much of the energy in popular Protestant anti-Catholicism was channeled into the interest group politics of the Protestant League, whose activities have recently been carefully analyzed by Helmut Smith (1995). According to Smith, the Protestant League was founded in 1887 to continue the cultural struggle against Catholicism and to rid Germany of ultramontane influences. The League gained over 500,000 adherents, making it Germany's largest Protestant lay organization and one of the nation's largest organized interest groups overall. The Protestant League identified its chief enemy as the Catholic Center party, yet the League itself fielded no candidates; the League offers an early example of purely negative campaigning. In addition to opposing the Center party, the League's activities even included financing the quixotic "Los von Rom" movement to convert Austrian Catholics to Protestantism in a failed paroxysm of pan-German integral nationalism. Despite its claim to represent all of Protestant Germany, the League's supporters were highly concentrated in densely urbanized areas of mixed confession, such as the large cities in the Rhineland. In sum, the Kulturkampf perversely provoked the modern political organization of Catholics without a corresponding centralization of Protestant political representation, not to mention any organizational benefit to liberals.

The Kulturkampf was an equally great failure in encouraging liberal or Enlightenment forms of religiosity among the Catholic population. It is not coincidental that the campaign against Catholicism was matched by a growth in Marian visions. In his analysis of the outburst of mass religiosity in Germany of the 1870s, David Blackbourn emphasizes the confluence of forces that contributed to aspects of the Marian apparitions—from economic crises and social and demographic change, to the increasing Romanization of the Catholic Church, to the feminization of Catholicism, to local conflicts among villages, to imitation of other leading cases, especially Lourdes, and to clerical attempts to mobilize and control popular religiosity. But foremost among all the many factors at work in the Marian visions, according to Blackbourn, especially in their timing and their ability to capture the imagination on a mass scale, was the Catholic response to anticlerical liberalism and the growth of state power

84   Origins of Liberal Dominance

(1994 [1993]). The assault on Catholicism—fully supported by most liberals—engendered more backlash than new support; some of the backlash came in the form of quasi-political popular religious movements, such as the pilgrimages to Marpingen. In religion, as in politics, a powerful effect of the Kulturkampf was to encourage religious revival on a mass scale. Any account of German political development must therefore recognize that the nineteenth century simultaneously saw the creation of secular institutions of political mobilization, vibrant religious revival partially under clerical control, and the emergence of a religious political party that became increasingly autonomous from the Catholic Church.

Conclusion

Authoritarian political regimes in most of the German lands weathered liberal reform efforts in 1830 and 1848. As broad political participation became more institutionalized in the 1860s, liberals challenged authoritarian practices, but did not succeed in installing liberal reforms. In the most powerful German state, Prussia, for example, liberals tried but failed to liberalize the constitution. National Liberals accepted a junior position in the newly unified authoritarian government of the Reich in the 1870s and supported the cultural struggle against the Catholic Church. Liberals lost much of their influence in government in the 1880s and 1890s, even as parliament continued to function in a quasi-constitutional fashion with the active participation of other parties. While scholars debate the extent to which the Center Party served as a "functional equivalent" of a liberal opposition, the Center Party's organizing success deprived liberals of their own ability to earn support from a substantial fraction of the German electorate.

The structures of religious and political authority, especially the Protestant state churches, the changing bureaucratic links between states and the Catholic Church, and mass social and political movements oriented to religious issues in Germany, played critical roles. The Prussian state church rewarded conservative religious leaders who sought to turn Protestant churches into agents of antiliberalism. Leading dissidents in the church were disciplined and eventually forced outside of the established religious institutions. Two conditions had to be satisfied for the established churches to work against liberalism: First, the state had to control the resources of individual clergy and their ability to lead parishoners. Second, a coherent conservative ideology had to be worked out, according to which conservative clerical elites could discipline individual clergy. With both of these conditions satisfied, the Protestant churches worked against the liberal political movement.

The Catholic Church carried out its own political agenda in response to changes in the state in Germany. Before 1866, the Catholic Church encountered periodic friction with the Protestant ruling house in Prussia, but the church largely sought to work within the state and discouraged independent political activism. The Catholic Church's response to the changing political situation took place both at the highest levels of church-state interaction and at the local level in terms of church encouragement of new forms of popular religiosity. After the 1866 military defeat of Catholic Austria, the church had no reasonable hope of an alternative state elite in Germany that would defend its authority and the direct assault on the institutional authority of the church intensified; given this new situation, the church encouraged new forms of political organization and participation.

Chapter 5

Successful Reform and Supremacy in Switzerland

Liberal dominance in Switzerland was unmatched anywhere on the Continent. Liberals began to control governments in the largest cantons of Switzerland in 1829–31 and extended this predominance to the federal level in 1848. The Radical party, Switzerland's mainstream liberal party, received more votes than any other party in every legislative election from 1848 to 1917. This level of popular support, combined with a majority representation electoral system, gave the Radicals an outright majority of the seats in the national legislature after 17 of the 23 elections between 1848 and 1914 (and never less than 42 percent of the seats) (Gruner 1978, 3:398, 470–79). Switzerland had a collegial executive, the seven-member Federal Council: all seven seats went to liberals on the councils between 1848 and 1891; six liberals and just one conservative sat on the councils from 1891 to 1914.[1] Liberals remained a central political force in Swiss politics long after liberal parties elsewhere in Europe were much reduced in power; Swiss liberals finally introduced proportional representation and conceded just over a fifth of the vote to the Social Democrats in 1919.

The early and comprehensive victory of Swiss liberals was held in high esteem in southwestern Germany and elsewhere in Western Europe. In the 1830s and 1840s many German radicals and political fugitives sought refuge in Switzerland, where liberal publicists evaded censorship in their home countries. Democrats, nationalists, and other dissidents found temporary haven in Switzerland, including Giuseppe Mazzini and Louis Napoleon, for example (Craig 1988, 84–89; Steinberg 1976, 31). The victory of Swiss liberals in 1847

---

1. Party representation in the Federal Council was as follows (Conrad 1970, 68).

1848–91	7 Liberal
1891	6 Liberal, 1 Conservative
1919	5 Liberal, 2 Conservative
1929	4 Liberal, 2 Conservative, 1 Peasant
1943	3 Liberal, 2 Conservative, 1 Peasant, 1 Socialist
1953	4 Liberal, 2 Conservative, 1 Peasant
1954	3 Liberal, 3 Conservative, 1 Peasant
1959	2 Liberal, 2 Conservative, 1 Peasant, 2 Socialist

over their conservative, Catholic opponents—in defiance of great power conservatives from Metternich to Guizot—"had an electrifying impact on liberals everywhere," first in Sicily and Naples, then in Paris (Holborn 1969, 3:47).

This chapter describes the character of Swiss liberalism and investigates the contributions to liberalism made by the interaction of the liberal movement with state and religious institutions. Switzerland's Protestant churches were tied to local institutions of political power, rather than a territorial state or Rome, and could not be turned into effectively antiliberal agents. Antiliberal religious movements in the Protestant world, such as Pietism, did not find support in a landed elite or state church in Switzerland. Pietist reaction to liberal advances did occur, but it was severely limited by the lack of powerful class or institutional support. For the most part, liberal movements themselves could capture Protestant institutions and turn them to political advantage. Protestant churches under liberal control generally supported the liberal program, especially when it came to combating the influence of the Catholic Church in Switzerland. The Catholic Church proved to be the greatest obstacle to the liberal movement and also a great provocation to unity within the liberal camp.

City Domination in a Confederal State in 1815

Switzerland's "cellular" political structure lacked a territorially aggrandizing center, a large taxation bureaucracy, or permanent military apparatus of its own. Twenty-two cantons comprised the Swiss Confederation in 1815.[2] A long and complicated history of seeking refuge from military threats and of acquiring international recognition for their sovereignty had placed the various cantons in a loosely connected political entity. The individual cantons exercised authority in all matters save foreign policy, which was assigned by the Congress of Vienna to a weak confederal government. The confederal government did not even have a permanent capital; it rotated among three important cantons, Bern, Zurich, and Luzern, every two years. The head of government in the director-canton automatically became president of the Confederation. The for-

---

2. The Congress of Vienna of 1814–15 returned Switzerland to the confederal system of the ancien régime (abandoning the relatively centralized constitutional framework that had been adopted under Napoleon's direction). The twenty-two cantons comprising Switzerland included two pairs of "half-cantons," Obwalden and Nidwalden, and Appenzell Außerrhoden and Appenzell Innerrhoden. Each half-canton received half the number of seats in the senate as a full canton. Basel split into the half-cantons Basel-City and Basel-Country in 1833 (a 1969 vote in Basel-City and Basel-Country rejected a proposed reunification). A 1974 plebiscite removed the Jura district from Bern and made the Jura a separate canton.

TABLE 6. Institutions, Reform Dynamics, and Outcomes in Switzerland

Elite Phase

State and Church Institutions at Onset of Liberal Reform	*Non-liberal, churches not incorporated* Weak confederation of oligarchies; each canton has established Protestant church or allied Catholic church	
Liberal Policy toward Religious Authority	*Preserve* Retain Protestant church authority	*Attack* Curtail Catholic Church authority
Response of Clergy	*Support* Aid liberals	*Opposition* Secede and seek alliance with monarchs
Fate of Elite Liberal Reform	**Successful** Liberal constitutions in most cantons in 1829–31; Catholic secession suppressed in 1847; national constitution in 1848	

Mass Phase

Institutions at Onset of Second Liberal Reform	*Parliament sovereign* Each canton has established Protestant or increasingly autonomous Catholic church	
Liberal Policy toward Religious Authority	*Preserve* Retain Protestant church authority	*Attack* Curtail Catholic Church authority
Response of Clergy	*Support* Aid liberals	*Opposition* Aid prochurch politicians
Provincial Middle-Class and Peasant Reply	*Support liberals* Protestants support Radical party	*Oppose* Catholics support Catholic party
Party and Regime Outcome	**Supremacy of Liberals** *Strong liberal parties in constitutional democracy* Radicals dominate Protestant cantons and national government, but Catholic parties strong in Catholic cantons	

mation of the Swiss Confederation was thus a bottom-up process that was ratified by other European powers.

Political authority in the cantons was exercised according to the dominant conservative ethos of the post-Napoleonic era in Europe. A Swiss political theorist, Carl Ludwig von Haller of Bern, articulated the philosophy of the conservative governments. Haller called for the return to the general law of nature, in which the more powerful ruled and the weaker found support in the stronger; he outlined government in accordance with the order of God, and the right of rulers to rule distinct from any right of the people. He based his ideas not just on the history of the middle ages, but also on his observation of the patrician families of Bern (Bonjour, Offler, and Potter 1952, 242–43). In line with these ideas, the Restoration in Switzerland gave exclusive political power to the leading aristocratic families in each canton. The Swiss confederation, in other words, sought to turn back many of the advances spawned by the French Revolution of 1789.

Urban oligarchies ruled most Swiss cantons. Government in the cantons of post–Napoleonic Switzerland granted effective sovereignty to a closed caste of urban oligarchs and placed every other member of the society in a subject status. The Restoration political systems in Swiss cantons with cities took two characteristic forms, patrician and guild. In both, the cantonal government was formed by a Small Council, which acted as the executive, and a Great Council, which typically had a broader membership. Offices in the Small Council were typically lifetime appointments and vacancies were typically filled according to the wishes of the remaining members. Under the Restoration, power resided in the more exclusive Small Councils rather than the Great Councils. The end result was essentially the same in patrician and guild cantons: a small, urban elite monopolized political power.[3]

---

3. Scholars disagree over the significance of differences between patrician, guild, and even assembly cantons. Martin emphasizes the similarities among these types.

> It hardly matters whether this administrative class was recruited on grounds of birth, as at Berne, Lucerne, Solothurn, and Fribourg, whether it was composed of the leaders of certain privileged guilds as at Zurich and Basle, or whether it was a plutocracy which could offer a higher bid for the posts, as happened in the smaller cantons. In practice, the administrative class was everywhere drawn from the wealthiest members of the population and they invariably recruited themselves, by co-opting further members. The diversity of forms only served to mask identically similar results. The aristocracies came into being in exactly the same way as the peasant dynasties and corporative oligarchies. (1971, 128–29)

Dändliker argues for differences: The assemblies in small cantons limited the development of ruling families; strong guilds in Zurich, Basel, and Schaffhausen likewise slowed the concentration of political power in the hands of just a few individuals; the aristocratic seizure of power was most thoroughgoing in Bern, Fribourg, Solothurn, and Luzern (1899, 169–70).

Most cantons were effectively dominated by the largest city or town in them. The Restoration cantonal regimes provided for unequal representation of urban and rural populations in cantonal councils. Typically a capital town provided two-thirds of the representatives to the cantonal council and the countryside the remaining one-third. Yet the sovereign towns were outnumbered by more than ten to one in terms of population. Four Protestant cities, Zurich, Bern, Basel and Schaffhausen, with together somewhat over 40,000 residents, ruled over more than 600,000 people. Four Catholic cities, Luzern, Zug, Freiburg and Solothurn, with together about 15,000 residents, ruled over 190,000 people. The city of Bern, with a population of about 10,000, ruled over a cantonal population of over 400,000. The representatives of the countryside in the Great Council numbered 99 out of 299 (even these figures overstate rural representation, for rural representatives rarely took part in the debates). In the more important Small Council, rural members occupied just two out of 27 seats. Swiss cities, despite their small size, thus dominated the surrounding countryside.

A third form of cantonal regime, a *Landsgemeinde* (assembly), was present in a few cantons with small populations and no large towns. These regimes upheld liberty and equality in the classical rather than modern sense (*pace* Benjamin Constant). The assembly cantons operated on the principle of direct democracy. An assembly of all adult males met once a year to debate and decide upon policies, offices, taxes, spending and intercantonal politics. These cantons did not sharply distinguish between town and country in terms of political rights. They had overwhelmingly rural residential patterns and Catholic populations. They included the two half-cantons of Obwalden and Nidwalden, the two Appenzells, Uri, Schwyz and Glarus, with a total of 157,000 residents in 1837, or just 7 percent of Switzerland's population (Comité pour une Nouvelle Histoire de la Suisse 1983, 2:186, table 2). Uri, Schwyz, and Unterwalden formed the historic core of Switzerland, dating back to their joint declaration of sovereignty against the Hapsburgs in 1291, but in their political structure they were more the exception than the rule in a confederation whose strongest members were essentially urban oligarchies.

Established Churches and Confessional Divide in 1815

Churches were enmeshed with every canton's political structure. They were essentially "canton churches," established in each locality. In the cantons that became Protestant, the reformers had sought protection under political structures. In Zurich, the former parish priest Huldrych Zwingli led the Reformation in a direction quite congenial to the secular authorities:

> For some time the Great Council had, without challenging the spiritual authority of Pope and bishop, been concerning themselves with the administration of church properties and the competence and morals of the clergy and had gradually been taking over control of monasteries, prebends, and church courts and assuming the right to appoint the preachers in churches like the Großmünster. Zwingli not only welcomed this as a means of freeing the clergy from worldly concern and enabling them to concentrate upon their religious functions but wished to have the council assume ultimate authority for changes in church dogma and ritual as well. (Craig 1988, 14)

Zwingli's ideas and practices spread rapidly through the more urbanized areas of Switzerland and were mirrored in Calvinist Geneva as well. The religious division was laid down when the Forest Cantons, along with Zug, Luzern, and Fribourg remained Catholic. Zwingli himself died in a war that failed to convert the Catholic cantons, at Kappel in 1531.

Continuing and bitter religious wars among the cantons solidified the integration of political and religious authority in each locality. The First War of Villmergen (1655–56) ended in victory for the Catholic cantons, and preserved the sovereign rights of cantons, including the right of a canton to enforce conformity to whichever religion it chose for its subject territories, several of which were urban areas under Catholic cantonal administration. The Second War of Villmergen (1712) overturned this result: subject areas of the Catholic cantons were granted religious liberty to change their confession and several such territories passed over to the control of the Protestant cantons. One key result of these wars was that cantonal organization came to reflect confessional differences more closely; a second key result was the division of Switzerland along confessional lines with no clear central authority (Baker 1895, 337–54).

The near dominance of one confession in each canton, according to the electoral districts of 1851 (except where noted), shows the close match between canton and confession.[4] Ten cantons or half-cantons were Protestant, typically with far more than 75 percent Protestant population in all electoral districts: Zurich, Glarus, Basel-City, Basel-Country, Schaffhausen, Appenzell

---

4. The following data are adapted from Gruner 1978, 3:table 15, "Konfessionelle Gliederung (Anfangswerte)," 448–49, read in conjuction with table 16, "Historische Wahlkreisnummer," 450.

Außerrhoden (1872), Thurgau, Vaud, Neuenburg, and Bern (99 percent or more Protestant in five districts, 37 percent Protestant in sixth district). Eleven were Catholic (typically far more than 75 percent in all electoral districts): Luzern, Ticino, Valais, Freiburg, Solothurn, Appenzell Innerrhoden (1872), Uri (1872), Schwyz, Obwalden (1872), Nidwalden (1872), and Zug. Only three were mixed with a Protestant majority: Graubünden (53 percent Protestant), Geneva (54 percent Protestant), and Aargau (98 percent, 54 percent, and 12 percent Protestant in three districts). Just one was mixed with a Catholic majority: St. Gallen (54 percent, 68 percent and 63 percent Catholic in three original districts).

The churches and the modern Swiss state had virtually no connection. Federal institutions emerged only in the nineteenth century, well after religious institutions had formed their tight connections to cantonal governments. France's invasion in 1798 and Napoleon's imposition of a confederal political structure in 1803 established the first modern national institutions. As could be expected from the heir of the Revolution of 1789 and signer of the Concordat with the papacy in 1801, Napoleon made no provision for the creation of confederal religious institutions but instead respected the existing religious differences. The second great step in the formation of the modern Swiss state was also not designed to build religious institutions along with the new political institutions. The federalist forces that defeated separatist cantons in the brief civil war of 1847 were concerned primarily to curtail Catholic resistance to national integration. In the constitution-writing of 1848, federalists curtailed the institutional authority of the Catholic Church and established a few secular institutions, but did not impose Protestant churches on the Catholic territories. The Swiss state was thus formed without a parallel set of religious institutions.

Liberalism from Restoration to Regeneration, 1815–31

Swiss liberals shared the standard liberal vision of constitutional and parliamentary government and pressed for the same fundamental rights enunciated by French republicans. The liberal reform program by 1830 included political rights for adult males (but with the crucial distinction between "active" and "passive" citizens), direct elections of the members of the cantonal legislatures for fixed terms, separation of legislative, executive, and judicial powers, publicity of debates, liberty of the press, protection of individual liberty and property by law, and the right of petition (Baker 1895, 477). Liberal movements in Switzerland therefore sought to promote constitutionalism, parliamentary government, formal sovereignty of the people, and active political rights for the elite strata of the middle classes excluded from power under Restoration regimes. The desire for a fair representation of urban and rural interests in government formed a central element of the liberal vision of constitutional and parliamentary government in Switzerland. As for the second typically liberal goal of economic individualism, the early Swiss liberal movements sought to free the economy from guild restrictions and to abolish intercantonal tariff barriers. The anticlerical goal had not yet resulted in a Protestant versus Catholic struggle, since most cantons were religiously homogeneous and power was still located at the cantonal level. An important liberal movement among Catholics within Catholic Switzerland, especially in the leading Catholic canton, Luzern, sought to limit the authority of the clergy to the realm of religion.

The early liberal movement sought to create a stronger national government and more active national feeling among the people. Among the many organizations that sought to promote national feeling beginning in the 1820s was the national shooting society. The society limited neither its membership, which was open to all Swiss men, nor its mission, which went beyond marksmanship. The society sought to deepen the ties between Swiss citizens and foster the sentiment of national unity, as Article 1 of its constitution declared. Other national societies included the Swiss Society for Natural Sciences (which brought together professors from around the confederation), the Zofingen Society (a society of students united by science and patriotism), and Federal Societies for singing, gymnastics and medicine. The assemblies of each of these societies were political events, "implicit protest[s] against the abuses of cantonalism" (Martin 1971, 214). Among the most important of these assemblies were the five national shooting competitions. The first Swiss shooting competition took place in Aarau in 1824. The Confederation's Shooting Society organized confederal competitions thereafter in Basel (1827), Geneva (1828), and Freiburg (1829) (Biaudet 1977, 914–15). The society's fifth competition, in Bern in 1830, coincided with the meeting of the Confederal Diet in that city and brought a large audience just outside the city walls. Representatives of the conservative regime in Bern received a cold reception, while prominent liberal speakers enjoyed hearty applause (Junker 1990, 2:17–18). Liberals envisioned a strong central government to replace persistent rivalry among the cantons and interference from foreign powers such as Austria, Prussia, and France.

In large part, these liberal movements proved successful, as liberals established constitutional regimes in most cantons from 1829 to 1831. By 1831, new liberal constitutions were put in place in Switzerland's eight most populous cantons and three smaller ones, altogether including about three-fourths of the total population of Switzerland (in Zurich, Bern, Luzern, Freiburg, Solothurn, Schaffhausen, St. Gallen, Aargau, Thurgau, Ticino, and Vaud) (Craig 1988, 45). The liberal cantonal constitutions transferred power from the Small Councils to the Great Councils, ensured equitable representation of rural and urban areas, and called upon the people as the sovereign power in ratifying these changes. The goal of national unity, both in the conditions for intercantonal trade and in the growth of national political institutions and building national feeling, proved harder to achieve: liberals failed in several attempts in the 1830s to strengthen the national government.

Liberal Movements in the Cantons

The main centers of power were cantons and liberal organizing took place at the cantonal level. Some cantons, by virtue of their larger population, greater economic development, or position of political leadership exercised more influence in the confederation than other cantons. Bern and Zurich had the two largest populations: Bern's population of 408,000 was more than twice that of any other canton except Zurich's 232,000. Luzern, although it was only the sixth largest canton in terms of population, ranked third in terms of political influence behind Bern and Zurich. As the largest canton with a predominantly Catholic population, Luzern's leaders often spoke for the 40 percent of the total confederal population that was Catholic. The Papal Nuncio's residence in Luzern symbolized the church's view of the importance of that canton in Swiss politics. Since the fate of Swiss liberalism depended on its performance in these three most important cantons, it is worthwhile to trace its development in them first, and then consider cantons that provide informative contrasts.

Liberal Movements in Three Influential Cantons

Reform in Zurich indicated the rural-urban alliance that underlay the liberal movement. The impetus for reform came from the middle classes in the countryside, from the communities on the lake shores, and from the middle classes in the city of Zurich itself. Opposition to the patrician regime united these middle-class reformers. This is the sort of liberal movement that could be formed when religious institutions did not divide rural and urban areas.

The area around the lake of Zurich typified the Swiss pattern of extraurban economic development. Most of the population lived in small communities. There was no community over 10,000 people outside of the city and just 10 percent of the population lived in communities of middling size (9,999 to 5,000 inhabitants), while fully 65 percent lived in small communities (4,999 to 2,000) and 25 percent in extremely small communities (1,999 and under).[5] Yet much of the work force, according to the standard measures, had moved out of the agricultural sector and into the service and industrial sectors of the economy. In 1872 (when data are first available for the district outside of the city), just 31 percent of the work force was engaged in agriculture, while 60 percent were in services and 9 percent in industry (Gruner 1978, 3:448). These areas were not urban, either in the sense of the size of their populations or in the sense of the privileges associated with having a sovereign municipal government, but their residents included many members of the nonagricultural middle classes.

Residents of these rural but economically advanced areas promoted liberal reforms. "An assembly of councillors from the rural district held at Uster in October [1830] formulated very moderate demands as to the revision of constitution required by them, and still yielded precedence to the town in the matter of representation" (Dändliker 1899, 248).

Yet the reform movement from the countryside provoked fear in the city. The demands issued by some rural political organizers unnerved middle classes. Pamphlets circulated in the canton calling for as many as three-fifths of the seats in the Great Council to be held by the representatives of the countryside. "This alarmed the city liberals . . . who were not immune to the common urban fear of *Bauernregiment,* and it seems to have aroused caution among some of the lake dwellers as well" (Craig 1988, 45). In other words, the liberal reform movement appeared strong, and therefore threatening to some, because of the assumption that peasants sympathized with the cause. At the same time, peasants were not organizationally integrated into the movement itself, even the middle classes mistrusted the political behavior of peasants. Peasant participation was assumed to be likely to take a traditional form, the peasant uprising, which was a threat to the existing regime but not the basis for a stable pattern of political participation. In this way peasants can be seen as silent partners in an otherwise elite coalition to transform Restoration regimes in a liberal direction.

This rural reform movement quickly acquired leadership and direction from the urban, professional middle class. In this case, a German professor who had been banished for his activities in the reform movement in Germany in 1817–20 and who was in Paris during the Revolution of 1830 exercised

---

5. These data are for 1851 in the second electoral district in Zurich, which excluded the city and surrounded the rest of the lake (Gruner 1978, 3:448).

considerable influence over the reform movement. This urban professional reinterpreted the demands of the countryside in the terms of liberalism.

He allied himself to the zealous partisans of reform, fought for the liberty of the press, and endeavoured specially to influence Zurich, which he looked upon as the intellectual head of the Confederation. At the time of the revolution in Paris he met with some of the most influential citizens of Zurich upon the Rigi; their narrow-minded views of the reforms to be undertaken induced him to try to convert Zurich to the principles of equality of rights for the citizens of every canton, the sovereignty of the people, and popular education. He wanted to establish "Constitutional Councils" (*Verfassungsräte*), and was the first to use this expression (Dändliker 1899, 248).

It was left to this German professor, Dr. Ludwig Snell, to publish the wishes of the lake communities in a definite form. He wrote the "Memorial of Küsnach" in concert with the communal association of Küsnach. According to this memorial, the country district was to elect by universal suffrage two-thirds of the 212 representatives in the Great Council, who should thus form the representatives of the sovereign people; further requirements included the division of powers, publicity of administration, the abolition of the tax-based limited suffrage, the right of petition, and liberty of the press. The author of the Küsnach Memorial sought compromise on the question of representation in the Great Council by proposing only two-thirds representation for the countryside, with a provision for review at a later date (Craig 1988, 45). Even so, the existing Great Council, dominated by the old city administration, refused to accept these reforms.

Rural pressure proved essential in forcing the acceptance of these reforms. The pressure came in the form of another mass meeting, again, outside of the city at Uster. This assembly demonstrated popular support for liberal reforms. The assembly at Uster, at which 7,000 to 8,000 burghers were present, endorsed the program of the Küsnach Memorial (Craig 1988, 46). This "Day of Uster" made a powerful impression;[6] the government ordered the immediate election of a new Great Council. City liberals announced their support for the Uster resolution (Craig 1988, 46). The new Great Council drew up a new

---

6. Not all of the activities were peaceful. The workers of Zurich who had come to the popular assembly at Uster on November 22, 1832, "were incited to set fire to a spinning-mill, they probably . . . intended to express their hatred of the machine which took bread out of the workers' mouths" (Martin 1971, 210).

constitution for the canton that enshrined the central principles articulated by the urban, middle-class leadership of the liberal movement. The Great Council approved a draft that was then ratified in a popular referendum.

One of the first acts of the new government was to dismantle the physical barrier between city and countryside, the old city wall. Liberals sought to promote economic growth and free the city from its confinement. But they also sought to bring city and country together. As the Governing Council proposed to the Great Council,

> When these dark bulwarks against the countryside fall and friendly houses and gardens rise in their place, then gradually with this material barrier the mental one will also disappear, and the city and the countryside will extend the hand of brotherhood across the gulf that has vanished. (Craig 1988, 50)

Zurich, home of Zwingli in the sixteenth century, again took up the mission of bringing ideological uniformity to Switzerland in the nineteenth century's great movement of liberalism, as we shall see below. Liberalism was less demanding than Zwingli's Protestantism, but also more successful at building institutions outside of its original home.

The most active opposition to the patrician regime in Bern came from the towns and villages of the countryside. The center of this opposition was the canton's second largest community, Burgdorf, whose population was just 3,600 and less than 1 percent of the canton's total population as late as 1850 (Junker 1990, 2:170). The leaders of the opposition movement in Burgdorf nevertheless had solid middle-class credentials: of the three brothers at the head of the movement the eldest was a *Stadtschreiber* and member of the Great Council, the more radical middle brother was a notary and lawyer, and the youngest and equally radical was a professor of botany at the Academy in Bern (Junker 1990, 2:20–21).

A large proportion of the nonpatrician citizenry in the city of Bern supported the movement for a "regeneration" of the canton. Just 27,600 people resided in the city of Bern in 1850, or about 6 percent of the total population. Among the prominent urban leaders were respected jurists, just as solidly middle class by profession as the leaders from outside the city (Junker 1990, 2:170, 22).

Few patricians sympathized with the liberal cause. Among the few who did were those associated with educational institutions. The founder of the school in Hofwil, Philipp Emanuel von Fellenberg, was one such patrician; he earned the opprobrium of his peers as a traitor to his origins. Several sons of patrician families studying under the free-thinking professor Samuel Schnell also sympathized with the liberal movement. In general, however, the overwhelming majority of patrician families resisted liberal innovation, including the new constitution of 1831 (Junker 1990, 2:16; Gruner 1943, 134ff).

Economic factors contributed to the conflict between the patriciate and the middle classes. Patricians excluded nonpatricians from administrative posts in the government of the canton. In Bern the conflict between the middle classes and the patriciate had intensified since 1789, for Bern's loss of sovereignty over its subject territories (Vaud, Aargau) reduced the total number of available posts. Before 1789 many nonpatricians were able to gain bureaucratic posts; after 1815 patricians took all of the reduced number of available posts. Patricians recovered slowly from the economic hardships of the Napoleonic era. This forced an even greater gulf between patricians and their subjects, for many patricians sold their land in the countryside in order to maintain their style of life in the city (Junker 1990, 2:16–17).

In part the urban-rural alliance depended upon the separation of the urban working classes from the liberal movement. The new constitution proclaimed the equality of political rights for all males over twenty-three years old, which would seem to have invited radical politics, perhaps with the support of the working and lower-middle classes. But the constitution disenfranchised much of the urban working and lower-middle classes through a residency requirement which only the ownership of substantial property could waive (those living in their home community had the right to vote, those who lived outside of their home community had to own property worth 500 Swiss francs in order to vote and own 5,000 francs worth of property in order to stand for election (Junker 1990, 2:46–47)).[7] Moreover, the mechanisms for voting assured the continued influence of the middle-class elite. The referendum on the constitution (27,802 in favor, 2,153 opposed), for example, was voted on by each community, usually in the local church, voting openly and without paper ballots in a public meeting. Liberals in this way could satisfy the demands for self-government and representation from the countryside without at the same time opening the door to political power for the working classes.

---

7. As the head of the constitutional commission proclaimed:
Radicalism must be firmly opposed. One must protect oneself, as one seeks to correct the errors of the present constitution, from creating new and even more dangerous ones. Only moderation, not extremism leads to the good. Domination by the poor, by those who have nothing to lose, by those for whom firm law and sound police order have no interest, must be feared and prevented by all possible means. Property is the guarantee, property owners the foundation of an ordered state. Whoever wishes power and durability for the new order stands against the extremism of democracy. (Junker 1990, 2:47)

These restrictions did more than exclude the working class from political power, they provided the foundations for a political system dominated by the elite of the middle classes. The property requirements were beyond the means of many in the lower-middle class, such as shopkeepers and skilled artisans. The decision not to provide a salary for representatives also deprived peripheral and poorer electoral districts of the possibility of electing one of their own to the assembly. Only those with the leisure and resources to serve in the assembly could afford to stand for election. In effect, the new constitution of 1831 through its voting requirements, public ballot and unsalaried council gave power to an elite stratum of the urban and rural middle classes. The elite stratum that wrested power from the old urban patriciate also sought to prevent lower classes from taking advantage of the newly changed political situation. As Bern's leading historian concludes, "The Bernese Revolution is not the act of the whole people, but the work of an enterprising middle stratum" (Gruner 1943, 367).

Luzern was an industrializing and overwhelmingly Catholic canton with a patrician city administration. An important liberal reform movement developed in Luzern during the period of elite politics. Leadership for the liberal movement as a whole came from the city of Luzern. A minister from Luzern, Thaddäus Müller, served as the president of the Helvetic Society, Switzerland's most aggressively anti-Restoration political organization. Although opposed to excessive influence of the Catholic hierarchy, the liberal Catholic movement of Luzern was not opposed to the religion as such; its leaders were in favor of rationalist and Enlightenment forms of religion. Müller, for example, spoke out in 1821 against the "intrigues" of the church hierarchy, but not against the Catholic religion (Dändliker 1899, 244). These liberal Catholics took the "Josephine" view, as it was termed in the Austrian Empire, that the Catholic Church should be subordinated to the secular political power. The liberal Catholic movement of 1830 in Luzern was anti-Vatican, whereas the French liberal Catholic movement of Lamennais at the same time was ultramontane, but both movements eventually foundered on increasing opposition between liberalism and the Catholic Church in the latter half of the nineteenth century. Liberal Catholics reformed Luzern's constitution in 1829, as in another Catholic canton (Ticino), even before the energizing news of the July Revolution in Paris in 1830.[8] This reform nearly doubled the relative representation of the country (by reducing the number of councilors from 36 to

---

8. The remaining canton with early revisions in 1829 was Protestant (Vaud).

19 while preserving the eight seats reserved for the countryside); the franchise was extended only to Catholics (Dändliker 1899, 253).

Lessons from Cantons with Failed or Weak Liberal Movements

Contrary to what one might expect, the linguistic cleavages within Switzerland did not hamper the liberal movement in most cases, since liberal organizing took place at the cantonal level and most cantons were linguistically homogenous. In the linguistically divided cantons, the liberal movement spanned the linguistic divide. The liberal movement in Valais failed to unite because linguistic divisions overlapped with the urban-rural cleavage. "In the Valais, where the upper and lower divisions were different in language and customs, the former maintained its old supremacy by its greater power" (Baker 1895, 480). Several areas of Switzerland did not experience liberal reform movements in the 1830s, including Geneva and Graubünden (Baker 1895, 479). Liberal reforms had already taken place in Geneva. Given the existing political structures in these cantons, the pressure for increased freedoms was reduced (Biaudet 1977, 921).

Urban residents in two cantons—Basel and Neuenburg—could draw on additional sources of power to preserve their oligarchic status. An unusually strong established church in Basel and the royal sovereign of Neuenburg were the institutions that strengthened the opponents of liberalism in these two exceptions to the general pattern in urban Switzerland. Only with the aid of federal government and the cantons which had already gone over to the liberal movement did liberal movements in these cantons come to power.

The urban regime in Basel rested on an exceptionally strong set of ties between the Protestant church, the leading urban-aristocratic families, and administrative exploitation of the surrounding countryside. The 18,000 residents of Basel had secured a majority of representatives in the cantonal legislature, despite the fact that 36,000 people lived in the country districts. In 1830 the city agreed to submit demands for constitutional reform to a commission, which was the typical response of Restoration regimes. An equal number of deputies from the city and the country comprised the membership of the commission. But the commission's work was more favorable to the city than elsewhere and the eventual outcome more violent.

The grievances of the countryside included the issue of administration in addition to underrepresentation in the councils:

> the country districts, as in the case of other states, possessed a certain amount of local selfrule, but were supervised and controlled by the canto-

nal officials called bailies, who collected the taxes and customs, enforced the laws, and otherwise represented the city's authority. (Baker 1895, 362)

The post of bailie included a salary, but its chief reward lay in the opportunity to exploit the office and its subjects for personal reward.

The commission rejected what Stefan Gutzwiller and other representatives from the countryside had called for, a council with seats assigned in proportion to population. Instead, the commission recommended a reform giving just over half of the seats on the future council to the countryside. In the future council the countryside was to have 79 seats, and the city was to have 75. The election system called for guild elections to elect 30 city representatives and 34 countryside representatives, with the remaining 90 representatives chosen by districts divided equally between city and countryside (Teuteberg 1986, 296).

The rejection of the call for proportional representation by the commission and the council's refusal to lighten the tax burden of the countryside combined to incite resistance. Rural groups took up arms in January 1831 and attacked the city of Basel. The city successfully raised and provisioned a counter-reform militia, thus beginning a cycle of revolt and repression that lasted for two years. The conflict ended in 1833 only after the intervention of federal troops and several plebiscites. The canton divided into two, each half having the same rights as the other cantons of the confederation, but only exercising one vote instead of two in the federal council. Basel and several adjoining communes formed the new canton of Basel-city while the remaining communes formed the new canton of Basel-country (Baker 1895, 482–83; Dändliker 1899, 257).

Although the new constitutions in the two halves of Basel were liberal, the liberal movement in Basel-city was on the conservative side of the liberal family and opposed efforts to reform the national constitution in the 1830s (Basel-city worked against the Concordat of Seven for example). Only when the politically salient issue became the struggle against the Catholic Church did the city join the rest of the liberal movement.

The peculiar constitutional situation of the Principality of Neuenburg gave added strength and incentive to its privileged urban strata in resisting reform from the countryside. Neuenberg, although part of the Swiss Confederation, owed allegiance to the King of Prussia. In response to two armed attacks from rural areas, "the Royalists in the chief town took the opportunity to vote, on 16 February 1832, for the Principality's separation from the Swiss Confederation" (Martin 1971, 216). Elsewhere in Switzerland, of course, urban elites did not have recourse to a king in their attempt to resist liberal changes. Fortunately for the rest of the Confederation, the King declined the invitation to assist his principality in detaching itself from the prevailing liberal developments in Switzerland. Neuenberg was forced to adopt a liberal constitutional arrangement.

In general, liberal movements were absent from the assembly cantons. Liberal demands seemed irrelevant to the political systems of the assembly cantons. The practice of the *Landsgemeinde* obviated demands for regular participation from the middle classes, for the practice of yearly assemblies already provided that central liberal demand. In practice, of course, wealthy families with the means to purchase allegiance tended to dominate these assemblies, but there was no formal, legal discrimination in the exercise of political rights by men. Other factors in play also limited interest in liberal movements in these cantons: the agriculturally-based economy and the absence of large towns meant that the typically liberal industrial and urban middle class was quite small. The confessional make-up of these cantons, almost exclusively Catholic, probably did not account for the weakness of the liberal movement in the 1820s and 1830s. Other Catholic cantons—Luzern and Ticino—did have liberal reform movements in the 1820s and 1830s. As the anti-Catholicism of liberal movements in Protestant cantons became more prominent in the 1840s, the chances for liberal movements in the Catholic cantons understandably declined.

There was a liberal movement in a territory subject to the rule of an assembly canton. The circumstances that generated this liberal movement underscore the importance of the middle classes being excluded from political power in generating a liberal movement in the elite period. An important fraction of the middle classes in the territory of Schwyz was excluded from political participation. The right to sit in the yearly assembly of Schwyz extended only to those residents of the inner districts (Schwyz and Muotta) and not to its outer districts, Einsiedeln and Kussnach, over which the inner districts exercised sovereignty. Residents of the subject districts pressed for liberal reforms: they set up their own government in May 1832, held elections, and sent representatives to the federal Diet. The old sovereign districts responded with force a year later. An armed body from the sovereign districts occupied a key town in the liberated districts. A levy of federal troops ended this attempt to reassert inequality in the canton and forced the acceptance of a new constitution providing for political equality for adult men.

Liberalism Transformed by the Struggle against Catholicism

Despite the liberal victories of 1829–31, the Restoration Constitution of 1815 remained in force at the national level and many cantons with weak or failed liberal movements preserved their older political structures. The limits of liberalism under the conditions of elite politics were further demonstrated through the failure of the regenerated cantons to reshape the federal constitution in the early 1830s and the ouster of liberal governments in several cantons in the late 1830s and early 1840s.

Liberals sought to rewrite the federal constitution in order to achieve the basic economic objectives of liberalism, which included the creation of a free, national market for goods and services, and to complete their political reforms, which included revising unregenerated cantonal constitutions and fostering a national sentiment. Liberals sought a new national constitution that would allow the products from one canton to be sold in another, lift transit tolls, free citizens to relocate within Switzerland, create a uniform national legal system and standardize money, weights and measures (Biaudet 1977, 923).

The first proposal put forward by a special commission in 1833 to reform the national constitution along these lines failed to gain the support of the required 15 of 22 cantons. The conservative cantons opposed the proposal. In addition, the liberal cantons themselves divided on the issue, as Radicals thought the proposal too moderate and Federalists thought it too extreme. A second, more moderate proposal also failed, especially when it was not approved by referendum in Luzern, which had previously favored liberal reform. In sum, the elite, cantonally based liberal movement did not assemble a national coalition for liberal reform. They failed to do so at the elite level, and did not yet have the resources to build a mass movement with these objectives. The newly empowered liberal governments pleased, above all, the "educated circles," one historian writes, while the broad mass of people, especially in the countryside, were not moved. Leaders and followers with so little in common soon came to a parting of the ways (Biaudet 1977, 927).

Once the liberals came to power in a Protestant canton, the church largely fell in line behind the new cantonal authorities. In a few notable instances, however, liberal politicians paid too little attention to conservative Protestant sympathies. In these instances, the opposition was a relatively disorganized rural movement and a conservative urban elite. Clerical resistance to the liberal movement was fundamentally limited by the fact their positions depended upon government support; Protestant clergy played little role in any conservative reaction. In addition, the Pietistic, anticosmopolitan form of Protestantism that had proved a great challenge to liberals in Protestant countries throughout western Europe found its roots in the countryside among the conservative peasantry. The leading families were part of the urban patriciate and basically shared the cosmopolitan outlook of the liberal reformers. It is helpful to examine more closely the conservative movements that came closest to terminating the liberal advance in the Protestant cantons. Within Protestant cantons, conservatives emphasized the differences between urban liberals and their rural supporters. The canton of Zurich serves as an instructive example here—especially with the aid of Gordon Craig's book (1988)—although similar developments took place in the rest of Protestant Switzerland. The period of conservative reaction in Zurich lasted from roughly 1839 to 1845. The conservative reaction relied on an antiurban, fundamentalist religious sentiment in the countryside. Conservatives turned out the liberal cantonal government in Zurich in 1839. "The immediate cause of this unexpected turn of events was a more than usually maladroit case of flying in the face of conventional religious feelings" (Craig 1988, 53). In particular, the government appointed to the university chair in New Testament Theology a theologian whose major work "treated the Gospel narrative like any other historical record and rejected all of its supernatural elements as being the stuff of myths" (Craig 1988, 54). Other issues associated with the antiliberal sentiment, including the liberals' destruction of the *Schanzen* and introduction of child labor laws, also fed into rural dissatisfaction with the liberal regime. Conservative leaders mustered a *Landsturm* invasion of the city by over 1,500 armed men from the countryside; following the confusion a conservative majority on the Council took power. In sum, conservatives in Zurich ousted liberals by emphasizing the religious differences between the fundamentalist, pietist countryside and latitudinarian, freethinking liberals in the city. Conservative activists succeeded in forcing the liberal theologian's resignation and then pressed for a greater role for religion in all educational appointments. Their campaign against state schools ran into popular defense of local schools, however, and without a firm hold on a strong institution such as a powerful church, the conservative forces "melted away like snow in the spring" (Craig 1988, 59).

Conservatives also turned back the liberal advances in the one Catholic canton with a liberal government.[9] A populist priest, Joseph Leu von Ebersol, led a countercoup against the Liberal regime in Luzern in 1841. The new conservative government abrogated the liberal constitution in 1844 and authorized the Jesuit order to run the canton's educational system. Von Ebersol's mystical anti-Rationalism, violent tactics, and democratic movement based in the proclerical peasantry clashed with liberal Catholicism and, as we shall see, helped to polarize the Protestant and Catholic cantons.

---

9. This and a later paragraph about conservative Catholicism in Luzern are based on Steinberg 1976, 31 and 60.

Conservative Protestant reaction collapsed when the opposition of Catholicism and Protestantism became salient. Protestants closed ranks behind liberals, especially Radicals. The Radical party was a broad coalition party that brought together radicals of various stripes from Geneva, Vaud, and German Switzerland: "Radicalism drew its strength from the fact that it was a party without class or regional connotations. It represented big industry, commerce and agriculture all at once" (Martin 1971, 240). Confessional polarization worked to the disadvantage of conservative Protestants, who defended Protestant tradition against liberals seeking reform in all areas, including religion. Protestants in general, including those who had supported conservatives, united behind the liberals' attacks on the Catholic Church. Religious issues worked to the advantage of liberals once politics on the intercantonal, national level became salient. Confessionally heterogeneous cantons served as flashpoints for liberal organizing since the confrontations between cantonal administration and the Catholic Church were most direct. For example, the radical party came to power in Aargau and, despite armed Catholic resistance, dissolved the monasteries within it borders in 1841 (Steinberg 1976, 31).

Conservatives in Zurich, notably, came under serious attack when they failed to defend Protestant parties against Catholicism in other cantons. The conservative government in Zurich opposed the Aargau Radicals' closing of Roman Catholic cloisters in the spring of 1841. Thus, a conservative, Protestant government in Zurich had come to the defense of the Catholic Church in another canton. This issue dominated the election campaign of May 1842, which brought liberals back into the Council in numbers equal to the conservatives. The Catholic question persisted, this time as the conservative and Catholic government in Luzern handed over its institutions of higher education to the Jesuits. In Switzerland, as elsewhere in Europe, liberals considered the Jesuit order an anathema, as the apotheosis of Catholic obscurantism, intrigue, and subversion. Thus, while the conservative Protestant regime in Zurich defended Catholic actions in Luzern, Zurich liberals campaigned against the reintroduction of Jesuits into public life. In the spring of 1845 the Great Council responded to popular sentiment in the canton against the conservative defense of Catholicism and replaced the Government Council with liberals. The elections of May 1846 confirmed this move by returning 158 liberals and just 34 conservatives (Craig 1988, 61).

Conservative Catholicism accelerated the polarization between Protestant-liberal and Catholic cantons: gangs of radical volunteers, the Free Corps, attacked von Ebersol's Luzern in 1841; Catholic cantons formed a secret pact of mutual defense, the *Sonderbund,* that was illegal under the terms of the confederal constitution; Radicals took control of more and more Protestant cantons, with St. Gallen's election of a radical government in the spring of 1847 finally giving radical cantons an absolute majority in the confederal Diet. "The Diet declared the *Sonderbund* dissolved, demanded the expulsion of the Jesuits from all Swiss territory, and the promulgation of a new democratic federal constitution" (Steinberg 1976, 31).

The Diet voted in October of 1847 to dissolve the *Sonderbund* by force, and the *Sonderbund* cantons were still organizing their military defense when the federal forces attacked in November. In less than a month the federal forces occupied Luzern and compelled the surrender of the Catholic cantons.

The liberals took command of the new Switzerland. The new federal constitution of 1848 elevated the nation over the separate cantons. It restricted cantonal sovereignty by a strong federal authority. The federal government included for the first time a mechanism for representing individual citizens in national government. The National Council (*Nationalrat*) offered one representative for every 20,000 Swiss citizens. In a blow to Catholicism, the constitution forbade the Jesuit Order. But the constitution maintained the territorial integrity of all of the cantons and did not otherwise impose Protestantism on the defeated, Catholic cantons. Deference to the separate rights of the cantons was institutionalized in the Council of States (*Ständerat*), which included two representatives for each canton (with one for each half-canton). As in the United States' system, the concurrence of both the Council of States and of the National Council are required for legislation to pass. The referendum on the new constitution was approved in a popular vote with 169,743 in favor and 71,899 against. Breaking down these results, voters in fifteen and one-half cantons accepted while six and one-half rejected it (the cantons that had been in the *Sonderbund,* minus Freiburg) (Dändliker 1899, 273). These votes together represented 55 percent of those eligible to vote in what was formally a universal male suffrage system. The relatively light turnout has been attributed to confidence that the new constitution would pass (Ruffieux 1983, 13).

The main issue in Swiss politics immediately after 1848, the building of a railway system, allowed moderate liberals to predominate. By 1852 the federal Assembly decided to turn over the construction of the railway system to private enterprise, at least in part because the costs of building the network exceeded the resources available to the federal government. Planning for the rail lines ignited political conflict between the various cantons, not based on religion or language, but based on the regional advantages to be gained from rail construction. "What all these disputes ultimately boiled down to was the rivalry between two towns, Berne and Zurich, and between the radical views on one hand and the moderate views on the other of two men, Staempfli and Escher" (Martin 1971, 234). These battles receded in the early 1860s as the system neared completion.

The major battles of the 1860s and 1870s concerned revising the constitution in the direction of direct democracy. The radical wing of the liberal movement came to dominate the movement and the political system as a whole in the 1860s and 1870s. The Constitution of 1848 envisioned adult male suffrage, although in practice many potential voters were disenfranchised, especially workers who changed their residence (Gruner 1978, 1a:94–155). Article 63 of the Constitution stated that every male over age 20 not excluded from active citizenship by the canton in which he resided had the right to vote. Although Article 4 BV specifically prohibited the use of minimum tax payments to qualify for the right to vote, Article 63 left open many ways in which individual cantons could restrict the franchise, especially in the definition of residence.

Switzerland's version of the Kulturkampf combined an attack on the church with the drive to revise the constitution in the direction of direct democracy. The Radical party was able to use the issue of anticlericalism to split any opposition to its democratic reforms. The increasing conflict between the Catholic Church and European states helped to push Switzerland further down the path of reform. The syllabus of errors in 1864 provoked great response in Switzerland. It was not sufficient to cause a radical coalition with the strength to revise the constitution, however. An alliance of French-speakers and Catholics stymied efforts to reform the constitution by referendum in 1866 that would have permitted residents from other cantons to vote in cantonal and communal affairs. The assembly rejected plans to transform the half-cantons into full cantons, introduce the popular veto and referendum, directly elect the Federal Council, set term limits on Federal Councillors, and unify business and penal codes (Martin 1971, 234). By 1869, there were several democratic revisions of the cantonal constitution of Zurich (initiative, referendum, and the popular election of the government and State councillors), which was soon followed by similar reforms in Thurgau, Bern, Solothurn, Luzern and Aargau. The declaration of papal infallibility in 1870 again caused a great response. But a second attempt at a national constitutional revision (unifying the law and the army) failed in 1872, again as a result of the alliance between French speakers and Catholics. The more direct provocations came in 1873 when the pope appointed a bishop in Basel and a vicar in Geneva; Switzerland broke its formal relations with the Vatican. A third and final attempt to introduce democratic reforms to the constitution succeeded in 1874, however, by modifying the centralizing measures and strengthening the anticlerical aspects of the revision. As a result, the reform plan passed with only the Catholics in opposition. The radical party thus split the alliance of French speakers and Catholics that had stalled reform efforts in 1866 and 1872 (Martin 1971, 236–37). The issue that held together the radical coalition in 1874, just as in 1847, was the struggle to curtail the institutional authority of the Catholic Church.

Legacies of Swiss Liberalism

Despite the common exposure of small countries to world markets, Sweden, Norway, Denmark, the Netherlands, Austria, and Belgium all developed stronger corporatist institutions than Switzerland (Katzenstein 1984, 1985). The perspective offered in this book helps explain why Switzerland resisted the pressures for developing corporatist-style bargaining arrangements longer than the other small countries of Western Europe. Liberal hegemony in the polity reduced the governing opportunities for left and Catholic parties, which had been the strongest organizational supporters of corporatist bargaining (Wilensky 1981). As for the working-class left, the comprehensive liberal victory gave Switzerland a working-class organization that was exceptionally weak for an advanced industrial country. Much of the union movement was closely tied to the liberal party, which resulted in the emergence of one of Europe's weakest Social Democratic parties. The workers' movement allied with the liberals, the Grutli, impeded the formation of a truly socialist party. Thus, when corporatist-style bargaining did develop, it excluded labor to a degree unmatched in the other leading corporatist political economies.

The strength of liberalism can be seen in the ability of the main political parties to incorporate the working-class movement. In the closing decades of the nineteenth century the liberal movement attracted working-class allies and stifled independent working-class organization to a degree unmatched in western Europe. Rather than independent organizing, many left-wing politicians focussed on issues of direct democracy and proportional representation. Both of these reforms, in their long-term effects, aided the preservation of the status quo more than they aided changes in a progressive direction.

Some organizers did work toward an independent organization, but a considerable proportion of Socialist success at the polls was due to electoral alliances with the Radical party (Luebbert 1991, 50–52). Independent Socialist candidates did not fare well at the polls. Supporters of the right-leaning Liberal party increasingly shifted to the Radical camp; their fear of socialism was greater than their opposition to increased powers for the federal government, which had been a central theme of their appeal. More importantly, these right-leaning liberals did not abandon the liberal movement altogether and go over to the Catholic party (as right-leaning liberals in Belgium had done).

By the 1880s and 1890s it was clear that the working class was slow to develop independent organizations for political activity. Socialist and left liberal politicians, given de jure universal male suffrage, did not make the suffrage a key element of their programmatic difference with other liberals. To be sure, these groups sought the elimination of the de facto suffrage restrictions. More important to socialists than "one person, one vote" issue however, was the question of the representational system. The system of majority voting with multiple elections made it difficult for socialists to succeed at the polls. Election law required an absolute majority on a ballot in order to win a seat. Second and third elections were held among candidates who failed to achieve this level the first time around. This procedure minimized the ability of minority candidates to succeed. In 1890, for example, the Socialists received 3.6 percent of the vote and just 0.7 percent of the seats. By 1911, the Socialists received 20 percent of the vote, but just 7.9 percent of the seats. Meanwhile, the national assembly overrepresented Radicals. The Radicals in 1890 received 40.9 percent of the vote and 50.3 percent of the seats. In 1911, Radicals received 49.5 percent of the vote and 60.9 percent of the seats (Gruner 1978, 3:485).

The main political thrust of the Socialist party was the push for proportional representation. The single-member district, first-past-the-post system resulted in a significant discrepancy between the proportion of the votes received by the Socialist party and the seats it received in the Federal Assembly. The introduction of proportional representation indeed had the effect of increasing the representation of Socialists in the Assembly. The introduction of proportional representation in 1919 gave the Socialist party approximately the same percentage of seats in the national assembly as votes cast (23.5 percent of votes and 21.7 percent of seats) (Gruner 1978, 3:485). It also had the effect of rewarding the formation of a new party from within the Radical party. The radical party lost a large fraction of its rural wing with the formation of the Peasant, Trade and Citizen's Party (Bauern-, Gewerbe- und Bürgerpartei), essentially a peasant and bourgeois party, during the run-up to the election of 1919. The party formed to represent the interests of peasants and other groups disadvantaged by the liberal party's emphasis on export industry development. It sought to take advantage of the war-induced food shortages and translate these into concrete gains for peasants (Conrad 1970, 44–47). The Radical party lost its absolute majority on the Federal council as a result. The consequences for the Swiss political system were not dramatic, however, for the peasant party essentially followed the Radical party's policy proposals in any area that did not directly affect their interests (Martin 1971, 240). The actual practice of governing brought peasants and industry into coalition, whereas before 1917 the coalition had been formed within the Radical party itself. Moreover, as the Socialists increased in strength, all of the bourgeois parties sought unity despite party labels in the Federal Council.

Efforts by peasants to form independent political organizations were also slowed by liberal dominance. The first significant propaganda appeal to increase the representation of peasant interests in the federal assembly occurred in the election of 1866 (Gruner and Frei 1966, 2:91). There was always some degree of peasant representation, but it was small. Just 3.5 percent of the delegates to the federal assembly between 1848 and 1872 were agriculturalists by profession, and most of these were large landholders who did not work the land themselves. Middle-class professionals, by way of contrast, were extremely well represented: 51.7 percent of the delegates were lawyers, 13.8 percent were involved in commerce, 10.6 percent were doctors, architects or engineers (Gruner and Frei 1966, 2:Table 2, 173). In 1887 the number of peasant representatives overtook the number of large landholders. Peasant representatives in the National Council in 1887 organized themselves as a club. This organization drew mainly from the rural delegates of the Liberal party, but also included members of other parties, thus suggesting that peasant representatives were prepared to reach beyond existing party labels. The club remained, however, an association of like-minded parliamentarians, and therefore posed only a weak challenge to the existing parties. In sum, the fundamental alliance of peasants with middle classes came under only slight pressure toward the end of the century and remained largely intact.

The switch to proportional representation in 1919 aided organizations outside the liberal parties. The Socialist party garnered a slightly higher percentage of the vote in 1919 than in 1911, 23.5 percent, but considerably more seats than previously, a fifth of the total 21.7 percent. As is typical of proportional representation systems, however, the strengths of the liberal and conservative parties were also secured against further losses. The shift to proportional representation modified the liberal coalition, but did not break it. The coalition came to be increasingly a coalition made between organizations, rather than within a single organization. Leading peasant politicians formed peasant parties in several cantons in anticipation of the elections of 1919, the first held under proportional representation. Peasant politicians in the liberal party argued that proportional representation offered them a greater voice than their alliance within the liberal party. Peasant organizers argued that liberals had focussed too heavily on export industry and that the struggle with socialism, as evidenced by the general strike of 1918, had not been pursued with success (Conrad 1970, 44). Competition with the socialists helped to provoke this new grouping. The peasant parties[10] were strong wherever the Socialist party was also strong, notably in Bern and Zurich. The peasant parties garnered 15.3 percent of the vote, forming the fourth largest political grouping after the liberals, socialists and conservatives (Gruner 1978, 3:398). The formation of separate peasant parties did not substantially weaken liberal power, for they voted with the Radicals on virtually every issue.

If Switzerland was the most liberal European country in the nineteenth century, why was it not the most progressive afterwards? Part of this seeming paradox has been answered above, by analyzing the contributions of dominant liberalism to the weakness of independent working-class organizations. Liberal accomplishments in one era and with respect to one set of circumstances have more than once led to "status quo conservatism" in a later era. In my view, this is an overly broad criticism of liberalism when writ large (Arblaster 1984), but it can be seen to operate when institutional interests come into play. The city of Basel, for example, exemplified this process:

> Renaissance Basel welcomed the alien, the eccentric and the heretical with more insouciance than most other European cities. Basel naturally became the home of a native Swiss tradition of free thought and in the eighteenth century the Enlightenment took deeper root in Basel than in any other Swiss canton save Geneva. It is no coincidence that the radical moving spirit of the Helvetic Republic, Peter Ochs, and many of his most passionate supporters, were Baselers. (Steinberg 1976, 138)
>
> Yet Basel's closely integrated urban oligarchy, established church, and administrative regime resisted the extension of civic and political rights to the countryside more effectively than any other urban regime in the early nineteenth century and in the latter half of the nineteenth century provided a regional base for the most conservative wing of the liberal movement (Gossman 1994, 70–77). In Switzerland as a whole the conservative wing of the liberal movement lost in the 1870s to the more powerful

---

10. Peasant parties did not come together with a unified and national platform until 1936.

Radical wing, which pushed for the establishment of the initiative procedures, a democratic reform in its time.[11] But the irony of liberal advance and subsequent stasis was not exhausted, for the institutions of direct democracy held back yet another advance: A century later, in 1971, Switzerland became the last European state to recognize the right of women to vote in national elections; according to one scholar, this lateness "seems directly linked to the institutions of direct democracy" (Inglehart 1979, 137).

---

11. The various institutions of direct democracy shade into one another:
In speaking of direct democracy, we are referring to three different institutions: the obligatory referendum in constitutional matters existed since 1848; the optional referendum, in legislative matters, existed since 1874; and the initiative [which] was introduced in 1891. . . . In practice these distinctions have lost some of their importance. The right of initiative can only be invoked in constitutional matters. But no precise definition of the constitution exists, there is no criterion to distinguish it from the law, so these notions are purely formal ones. The people therefore can always make use of their right of initiative by framing their request in the form of a constitutional article. (Martin 1971, 237)

Chapter 6

Religious Institutions, Reform Dynamics, and Liberalism

The argument of this book is that church and state institutions have to be brought back into our understanding of the origins of liberal regimes. Church and state institutions shaped the types of strategies adopted by religious actors toward emerging liberal movements, determined whether and how liberal parties acquired broad-based support as the dynamics of reform unfolded, and ultimately influenced whether and how political regimes developed in a liberal direction. When clergy and their followers forged a coalition with a liberal movement, they provided critical organizational resources and key votes to liberal organizers and the liberal movement succeeded. When clergy opposed liberals, but were themselves opposed by the rural middle class and peasantry, religious actors unwittingly provoked the formation of a large liberal constituency. Thus, the responses of religious elites and of rural social groups to the emergence of liberals occurred in distinct ways in different countries and these differences help account for the variety of liberal experiences.

A distinctive focus on church-state relations in the nineteenth century isolates a variable that is critical to our understanding of liberal regimes, but that tends to be overlooked in other important and recent comparative-historical analyses. Leading accounts that look at political institutions at the end of the eighteenth century illuminate the early structure of liberal democracy in various premodern forms of constitutionalism and various types of military organization (Ertman 1997; Downing 1992). In contrast, although not in disagreement, this book lays out the sources of liberal democracy at work in the medium- and short-run over the course of the critical nineteenth century; similarly, this book emphasizes an institution, religion, that at crucial moments took on at least equal weight with other institutions in determining the fate of various attempts at liberal reform.

An emphasis on religious institutions balances any tendency to devote exclusive attention to economic factors, even such important factors as the varying effects of international trade. While it is true that generally rising levels of international trade between 1840 and 1914 interacted with abundant and scarce factor endowments in national economies to influence domestic political alignments, this interaction was neither the only cause of domestic political alignments nor in every case the decisive cause of domestic political alignments (Rogowski 1989, 60). The possibility that religious institutions and the cleavages they provoked could trump trade-based alignments emerged strongly in the case of France, where we saw that questions of regime and religion repeatedly overshadowed tariff debates. German liberals' inability to forge a broad-based coalition among peasants and middle classes stemmed at least as much from their difficulties on confessional grounds as on trade, especially in the 1830s and 1840s, when trade had yet to reach the levels of the later part of the century. Even in cases where religion and factor endowments overlapped, as in Switzerland and Belgium, one cannot predict whether liberals would emerge victorious without assessing the strength of the religious dimension: Swiss liberals remained dominant over Catholics while Belgian liberals succumbed to the Catholic Party not because of any economic differences in the makeup of the respective coalitions, which we saw were quite similar, but because of the relative strength of Swiss Protestantism and its anti-Catholicism in its national context compared to that of Belgian anticlericalism.

The comparisons made possible by examining the comprehensive liberal domination in Switzerland, the contested victory of liberals in France, their qualified defeat in Belgium, and their co-optation and defeat in Germany underscore crucial determinants of the liberal experience that the usual comparisons do not reveal. Comparing the Continental experience to that of the United Kingdom and its former colonies underscores the crucial role of the church-state struggle in framing the possibilities for liberalism. In all of the countries where states and the Catholic Church mutually posed direct and frequent threats to their respective institutions, as in the Catholic and mixed Catholic and Protestant countries on the continent, the varied institutional relationships between the church and the state proved decisive in the formation of liberal coalitions. When the Catholic Church's institutional authority was compromised under the old regime, as can be seen clearly in the Belgian experience, the church could play a crucial role in supporting a liberal movement and in bringing about a transition to a liberal political system. Looking to Switzerland helps to break down the myth of Swiss cultural exceptionalism; Swiss political development was framed by the same institutional forces that operated elsewhere. The Swiss example shows how the absence of an absolutist monarchy and nationally established church largely confined the religious reaction against liberalism to the Catholic Church.

The remarkably comprehensive liberal victory in Switzerland involved continuous liberal rule from 1830 in most cantons and from 1847 at the federal level. Coalitions between urban and rural forces spanning both elite and mass periods of politics made this victory possible. The coalition under elite politics brought together urban elites and rural notables, including professors, teachers, lawyers, doctors, other professionals, university students, and prosperous farmers. This coalition united on issues of civil rights for the middle classes, constitutional government, and liberal economic policy. The coalition was organized as a series of local coalitions. The coalitions existed on the level of individual cantons, each of which had its own government. Moreover, given the homogenous confessional status of each canton, the liberal grouping in each canton did not cross confessional lines. Thus, in a Catholic canton such as Luzern, Catholics dominated the liberal reform coalition. In a Protestant canton, such as Bern, Protestants dominated a similar coalition. The coalitions did not have to cross regional or confessional lines, since the cantons were effectively sovereign powers.

Under mass politics, this coalition expanded to include the active participation of the mass of independent peasants. This new coalition differed from the elite coalitions in that it was a truly national coalition. In crossing cantonal boundaries, the new liberal coalition excluded Catholics who had been central to elite coalitions. The building of a nation-state, which was understood to include the reduction of the Catholic Church's powers, was a central unifying goal of this mass coalition. The religious conflict was grounded in the institutional struggle between the Catholic Church and the emerging liberal state; it therefore trumped social cleavages not reinforced by such formal institutional conflict, such as language, economic development, and, for most of the century, social class. The ability of liberals to rely on religious conflict to solidify a coalition of Protestants—French-speaking and German-speaking middle classes, workers, and peasants—made possible their extended domination of the Swiss political system.

At the other end of the spectrum, Conservatives ruled Prussia and most of the other German states from 1815 to 1871 and in unified Germany from 1871 to 1919, while allowing liberals sometimes to occupy a tenuous junior position in the ruling coalition. The comprehensive defeat in Germany has been seen in both elite and mass periods. Unlike elite coalitions in Switzerland and Belgium, Catholics in Germany pursued their objectives largely through tactical alliances with conservative monarchs. In sum, under elite conditions, the religious institutions and their ties to monarchs in German states prevented upper-middle classes from uniting against monarchical authority. German monarchs could therefore resist pressures to submit to constitutional and parliamentary government.

By the time of the transition to mass politics, the mass of the Catholic population was inaccessible to liberal appeals. As in the rest of Europe, German liberals sought to weaken religious ties by using the power of the state to reshape clerical functions, especially in the education of the youth. This policy increased the isolation and organization of the Catholic faithful, as it did everywhere in Europe where the population was loyal to the church hierarchy. Liberals became less enamored of parliamentary sovereignty and especially of universal suffrage, as it became ever clearer that liberal forces would not dominate in a democratic system. The potential for a Catholic majority threatened liberals in the 1860s; Bismarck employed this fear during the constitutional crisis in Prussia. By the time the national question was settled with unification under Prussian auspices in 1870, peasants and other groups that had formerly sought alliance with liberals had turned to conservative elites.

French liberals suffered setbacks and renewed challenges over the course of the century. They ruled briefly under the Orleanist constitutional monarchy, lost strength during the Revolution of 1848 and the Second Republic, then collaborated with or opposed Louis Napoleon from 1849 through 1870. Liberals finally emerged in command in the 1870s when they provided the primary impetus behind the Third Republic. Liberals turned back several attempts to overthrow the republican system. In France, as we saw, neither the movement of religious dissent within the church, nor the church itself, joined with liberals in supporting a constitutional monarchy on a durable basis. In addition, when the church recaptured the dissenting movement by the late 1830s, the church regained the ability to mobilize many people in an era of extremely restricted formal political participation and rudimentary political parties. The reincorporation of former dissenters made the national church a formidable institution in early-nineteenth-century France and therefore an attractive ally for conservative liberals. With its organizational ability, the church helped to strengthen the position of conservative liberals seeking to maintain the restricted franchise. In the final years of the constitutional monarchy, renewed ties between church and state sustained a highly restrictive franchise against reform, thereby setting the stage for the Revolution of 1848 and the end of the first liberal experiment.

Later in nineteenth-century France, political movements oriented to religion were influential again, but with different leaders and a different effect. These new political movements, like some of their predecessors, sought to reduce the authority of the church in political institutions. Now, however, they were led by secular elites, not by clergy. We have seen, for example, the educational societies that provided the organizational network for the emerging Republican movement, especially among the middle classes. In addition, anticlericalism provided the symbolic frames of reference that structured the political orientation of peasants in a newly democratized political system. New economic issues, such as tariff questions, altered the government's economic policies, but did not fundamentally restructure the dense set of links between the state, parties, and political movements. In sum, political movements linked by anticlericalism laid down the structures that would shape French political development for many years to come.

Liberals in Belgium also had mixed success. Belgian liberals dominated elite politics. They formed a coalition with Catholics in 1830 to secure Belgian independence and jointly supported a liberal constitution. As tensions with Catholics increased in the 1830s and 1840s, liberals developed a political press and several active urban political associations. Liberals formally founded a national party in 1846 and ruled on their own for most of the years after 1847. The transition to mass politics hurt the liberal party, however. The transition to mass politics was evident in several areas: Urban working and lower-middle classes organized in support of franchise expansion in the 1870s. Catholic peasants organized after 1878. The political press found a wide readership beyond those with the franchise. Most political groups admitted members who did not yet have the right to vote. In the face of all these developments, especially Catholic organizing in the countryside, Liberals lost the election of 1884 and every election thereafter.

The Belgian liberals' defeat was mitigated by the Catholics' acceptance of several key liberal principles. The Catholic party shared the liberal commitment to private property and the free market. The leadership of the party, especially the old guard, opposed government intervention in the market (as, for example, in worker protection, in which Belgium lagged behind the rest of Europe). The party departed somewhat from liberal tariff policy by providing a measure of agricultural protection, but no more so than was typical of European countries in the 1890s (Gourevitch 1986, 75–76). Catholic leaders did have a hierarchical and communitarian view of society, but this implied the personal responsibility of the employer for his employees rather than state-run welfare. Employees, in return, owed deference and loyalty to their employer. Thus, in practical terms, the Catholic party departed very little from the economic policies of the Liberal party. The liberal defeat was also mitigated by the Catholics' co-optation of a substantial fraction of the working class. The Catholic party mobilized about half of the working class: by 1914 Catholic trade unions had 110,000 members to the Socialist trade unions' 125,000 (Luebbert 1991, 142). In this way, the Catholic party divided the political loyalty of the working class, constrained the opportunities for socialist organization, and permitted the party to pursue liberal economic policy without having to confront unified working-class opposition until the interwar years.

Within our four cases, we have distinguished two paths opening to liberal regimes in the nineteenth and early twentieth centuries: a coalition uniting clergy and liberal reformers constituted one path, while organized movements of secularism constituted the other. If we seek to examine a broader array of experiences, an important research question is whether other national experiences with liberal reform were also framed by these interactions between religious institutions, liberal movements, and states.

Revisiting the Origins of a Paradigmatic Liberal Regime:
The United Kingdom

Liberalism predominated in no country as it did in the United Kingdom in the nineteenth century. "Between 1830 and 1886, a coalition of anti-Conservatives known at various times as whigs, Reformers and Liberals was out of office for scarcely a dozen years and lost only two of fourteen general elections" (Parry 1993, 1). Liberals in the United Kingdom are often taken as the ideal nineteenth-century liberals, with their enthusiastic support for free trade, liberal economics, parliamentarism, responsible government, and religious freedom. It is not unusual for studies of liberalism to devote more attention to the United Kingdom than to any other country (Arblaster 1984; Hall 1987).

An analysis of what is often taken to be the leading example of liberalism, that in the United Kingdom, suggests that clergy and liberal reformers found many elements of common cause on the path to liberalism. As is well known, many factors contributed to the strength of liberalism in parts of the United Kingdom, but the story is not complete without the role of religious institutions and their interaction with liberal movements for the possibility for the reform of the state.

The liberal movement helped to build a mass basis for a regime that, in its elite phase, had already made a substantial transition from authoritarian monarchy. The United Kingdom was unique among European states in that it had a parliamentary monarchy already in 1815. Elected deputies—many of whom were chosen in contested elections—shared power with the nonelected monarch. Parliament could approve or reject the makeup of the government and its budget. The institution of citizenship in England had already emerged in the seventeenth and eighteenth centuries out of the complex interaction between state-led legal reform and local patterns of associational life (Somers 1993). The transition from elite to mass liberalism involved an expansion in the rights of the male populace to participate in national politics. At the beginning of the century the franchise was limited to about 10 percent of the adult male population and its effectiveness varied widely from one electoral district to another given great differences in the number of voters per district. With the Second Reform Act of 1867, about two-thirds of the adult male population received the right to vote. Universal suffrage for men and women was enacted in 1919.

Church-state relations favored the growth of political opposition. An established Protestant church with close ties to the state faced, by the beginning of the nineteenth century, well-organized dissenting Protestant sects. In addition, Britain had barely assimilated the Catholic Church in Ireland into its administrative apparatus, thus the Anglican Church in Ireland was in a privileged position with respect to the Catholic Church. An established church in the midst of religious pluralism created civil, political, and social disabilities linked to religion. Religious pluralism, not just in belief but in organization, provided the institutional basis from which to resist the established church.

The Anglican Church was closely tied to the state at the opening of the nineteenth century. The established church was the Anglican Church in England, Wales, and Ireland and the Presbyterian Church in Scotland. For example, a property tax was levelled on ratepayers in England and Wales, regardless of their religious affiliation, for the maintenance of parish churches of the Anglican Church. The Test and Corporation Acts of 1661 and 1673 required that holders of public offices subscribe to Anglicanism. Religious tests were also required for matriculation at Oxford and Cambridge; marriages and burials had to be performed according to Anglican rites; births and marriages had to be registered by the church. In more general terms, the Anglican Church exercised institutional authority over taxation, office holding, citizenship, education, marriage, birth, and death. The Anglican establishment created inequalities among citizens based upon religion; these inequalities provided the common interests for liberal organizers to emphasize.

A series of dissenting movements had already broken away from the Anglican Church. Dissenting or nonconformist movements included Quakerism, Sandemanianism, Unitarianism, Congregationalism, Baptism, Wesleyanism, and Methodism. These organizations of religious groups, separate from the established church, dated from the seventeenth century in England; they were, moreover, politically active (Fulbrook 1983, 102ff). Dissenters were prominent during the reign of Cromwell (1649–60) (Bendix 1978, 292ff). By the nineteenth century, these movements supported their own clergy and controlled their meeting places through ownership of local chapels. The political engagement of these groups varied, with the Wesleyans, Methodists, and Quakers sometimes refraining from political actions, while Congregationalists and Baptists were at the forefront of the "Voluntaryist" movement that sought to remove compulsion from the church regime (Ellens 1994:7ff).

Nonconformist Protestant sects served as organizational bases for the emerging Liberal Party (Breuilly 1992, 253). The leader of the Liberal Party, W. E. Gladstone, himself remarked that nonconformity was the "backbone" of British Liberalism (De Ruggiero 1959 [1927], 116). Religious organizations and their elites themselves motivated and mobilized supporters for the liberal movement. Liberal elites welcomed the support of clerical leaders and their congregations. Liberals explicitly championed religious interests in their mobilizing efforts; liberal programs offered promises to the religiously motivated supporters of the liberal movement (Bentley 1987, 37–38).

In addition, the Catholic Church was relatively unprivileged under the church regime. Catholics were politically excluded by the Test and Corporation Acts and were also required to tithe to the Anglican Church. The Catholic hierarchy was not positively linked to the state, unlike the situation in another Protestant state, Prussia, where the Catholic Church often received support from the state. Catholic priests in Ireland received no subvention from the state and they exercised no authority in public education (Parry 1993, 266). The Catholic Church was connected neither to the British state nor to the large landowners in Ireland, who were, for the most part, Anglican Englishmen. Thus, the Catholic Church was beholden neither to the defense of the state, nor to the defence of an oppressive, rural, political economy. The Catholic support for liberalism can thus be understood as a response to the unfavorable institutional situation it faced under the old regime. Resolving the question of church funds in Ireland, with its implications for the church in the rest of the United Kingdom, "was probably the most important single step in the formation of the Liberal party" (Parry 1993, 108).

The church-state regime strengthened liberal forces and also weakened the resolve of conservative groups to make a stand on religious questions. As Breuilly writes, "there did develop from an Anglican point of view, the idea that church establishment might actually undermine religious belief, especially where the church in question had only minority support" (1992, 253). The great leader of the Liberal party, W. E. Gladstone, was an Anglican who "passionately upheld the legitimate authority of the government and the church," but he sought to "shelter the church from the dangers involved in association with politics and political controversy" (Parry 1993, 247). Liberalism was institutionally represented not only by the Whigs, Reformers, and Liberals, but it also had a strong influence within even the Tory party. On a comparative basis, British conservatives were more influenced by liberal ideas than were conservatives elsewhere in Europe.

Although the regime remained strongly liberal, the fortunes of the Liberal party waned as the religious basis for a broad liberal coalition eroded. The disabilities of Catholics and Dissenters were dismantled over the course of the nineteenth century in a series of complex reforms. The church rate controversy was settled in 1868. In 1869 the Anglican Church in Ireland was disestablished, followed by disestablishment in Wales in 1920 and the compromise Church of Scotland Act of 1921. The resolution of these issues and the existence of a formally established church in England, with virtually no remaining institutional authority outside of the narrow field of religion, helped to dissolve the liberal coalition and, in the years after World War I, usher in Conservative party ascendancy. Even under Conservative rule however, the legacy of liberal success in the United Kingdom persisted in the form of a Labour Party that had emerged from within, rather than in opposition to, the Liberal party and in a Conservative Party that was strongly influenced by the liberal tradition.

Implications for Contemporary Democracies

Within Europe many long-term legacies of struggles for liberal reform derive from liberalism's varied success across the Continent and the striking differences in the fate of liberal institutions in different countries. For example, the degree to which liberalism was institutionalized within a state shaped different modes of working-class mobilization and incorporation (Marshall 1964, 71–72; Bendix and Rokkan 1977 [1964], 89–126; Lipset and Rokkan 1967, 1–64; Lipset 1983; Zolberg 1986, 450). Successful liberal movements attracted working-class political leaders, co-opted important fractions of working classes, spawned divided union movements, and offered multiple organizational foci for working-class politics. Weak liberal movements, in contrast, attracted fewer working-class allies and unintentionally fostered the conditions for working-class organizations that were comparatively free from the influence of liberal leadership. Liberalism thus fundamentally changed the conditions facing subsequent political movements and the resulting institutional legacy of liberal parties' success or failure endures in the different party systems of Europe (Rose and Urwin 1969, 1970; Shamir 1984; Inglehart 1977, 1990). In addition, differences in the dominance of liberal parties before World

War I strongly influenced the survival of democratic regimes in the difficult interwar period (Luebbert 1987, 1991; Berg-Schlosser and De Meur 1994, 263). De Meur and Berg-Schlosser confirm the importance of pre–World War I outcomes by finding that Germany and all of the other interwar breakdown cases in Europe lacked liberal-democratic systems before 1914 (1996, 445).

Liberal institutions around the contemporary world constitute equally important long-term legacies of the first successful transitions to liberal regimes. To paraphrase and modify Gianfranco Poggi's citation of Max Weber, it is the paradoxical peculiarity of Europe to have developed distinctive institutions— such as the liberal emphasis on the rule of law and the participation of the ruled in the process of rule—that nevertheless acquired universal significance beyond their original historical setting (Poggi 1978, 168n. 39). A recent wave of transitions to democracy thus makes the study of earlier regime transitions again of scholarly interest, from both a substantive and theoretical point of view. The substantive importance of the first liberal regimes derives from their role in establishing models for political institutions. In Belgium and Switzerland the institutional continuity is direct, as both countries retain modified forms of the constitutions adopted in 1830 and 1847. In Germany and France, the current constitutional arrangements date from 1949 and 1958 and reflect both the inherited experience of each country and borrowed elements from constitutions in reference societies. Similarly, many of the new democracies have revived old constitutions—in many cases also dating from the nineteenth century—and modified them to take account of previous difficulties and contemporary reference models.

The theoretical importance of examining regime transitions lies in the idea that the more recent transitions to democracy can be compared to the transitions to liberal regimes covered in this study, thus broadening the comparative reach of recent scholarship and enabling us to evaluate three themes across a wider selection of cases (Schmitter 1995a, 1995b). The first broad theme that connects the varied transitions centers on the complex of relationships between liberalism and democracy. Examining the so-called first wave of transitions and the antecedents to the first wave of transitions sheds light on two types of sequences for liberalization identified in the transitions literature: liberalization culminating in democracy and democracy culminating in the building of liberal institutions. In the first sequence, liberalism is seen as preparing the ground for democracy, albeit in a highly contingent fashion. Robert Dahl analyzed the sequence of sustained political contestation prior to political inclusiveness and argued that this sequence was conducive to the survival of the subsequent democracy and likely to be limited to the first cases of democratization (1971). In a similar vein, "liberalization" is viewed as the first step in the opening of a noncompetitive regime to limited opposition, parliamentary forms, and civil rights, falling short of full democracy (O'Donnell 1979, 8). A widely cited passage in the transitions literature defines liberalization as "the process of redefining and extending rights . . . that protect both individuals and social groups from arbitrary or illegal acts committed by the state or third parties" and democratization as "the processes whereby the rules and procedures of citizenship are either applied to political institutions previously governed by other principles . . . or expanded to include persons not previously enjoying such rights and obligations" (O'Donnell and Schmitter 1986, 7–8). Much of the transitions literature seeks to answer the question of when liberalization leads to a transition to democracy (Przeworski 1992, 107–16). The emphasis on liberalism, defined as contestation and civil rights, that may or may not be accompanied by democracy with full participation in national politics, is helpful in examining the first transitions to liberal systems.

This book considers several transitions to liberal regimes, some of which later developed into fully democratic systems. As we have seen, the early liberal regimes were not democracies: National and local candidates contested elections without the resources of permanent, extraparliamentary political parties. Electoral systems involved narrow suffrage, public voting, and/or indirect elections. Nonelected authorities still played key roles: constitutional hereditary monarchs or other nonelected authorities exercised discretion in naming cabinet ministers and also controlled important resources that were not subject to parliamentary control. Liberal regimes of the early nineteenth century, in short, were undemocratic by virtue of their embryonic parties, circumscribed political participation, and powerful nonelected authorities. Given these differences, some early and decisive changes from authoritarian to liberal systems do not qualify as transitions to democracy. Belgium made the transition to a liberal regime in 1830 but was not a democracy until 1919.[1] Switzerland made the transition to liberalism in 1848 but was not a democracy until 1878.[2] Similarly, a partially constitutional regime was supported by many

---

1. Dix 1994 and Przeworski and Limongi 1997 (173) date democracy in Belgium to 1919; Vanhanen 1984 (64) states that Belgium crossed the threshold of democracy in the decade of the 1890s.

2. Dix 1994 (97) dates democracy in Switzerland to 1878; Przeworski and Limongi 1997 (173) date it to 1875; Vanhanen 1984 (148) states that Switzerland crossed the threshold of democracy in the decade of the 1880s; Therborn 1977 and Stephens 1989 date democracy in Switzerland to around 1880.

French liberals from 1830 to 1848 in France, yet the transition to democracy in 1848 was aborted by a presidential coup d'état in 1851, and a successful transition to democracy did not take place until 1875.[3]

Resistance to democracy was more open than it is today. In Europe, the attainment of broad suffrage came about through the struggles within indigenous traditions during the "long century" of democratization from 1789 to 1919 and took so long precisely because some key actors among the old elites resisted democratization (Therborn 1992). Robert Dix finds that contestation antedated participation in fully two-thirds of first-wave democratic transitions (1848–1931) but only one-third of second-wave transitions (1942–68); whereas in none of the third wave democratizers between 1973 and 1991 did contestation precede participation (1994, 94). The common first-wave pattern of contestation prior to participation is no longer feasible, for democracy is "today the overwhelmingly dominant, and increasingly the well-nigh exclusive, claimant to set the standard for legitimate political authority" (Dunn 1992, 239). Nevertheless, the task of building liberal institutions is far from over.

The second sequence that is shared by some of the early transitions and the more recent transitions is the sequence of an electoral democracy developing into fully a liberal democracy. This is a topic of concern for scholars concerned with deepening and consolidating new democracies. In many of countries where free and fair elections with broad suffrage have become institutional norms, the extension of liberal rights equally to all citizens remains incomplete. As Guillermo O'Donnell argues,

> In many of the new polyarchies, individuals are citizens only in relation to the one institution that functions in a manner close to what its formal rules prescribe—elections. As for full citizenship, only the members of a privileged minority enjoy it. . . . Informally institutionalized polyarchies are democratic in the sense just defined. . . . But their liberal and republican components are extremely weak. (1996, 13)

Informal institutions such as patrimonialism and clientelism within an electoral democracy may reproduce themselves successfully and prevent the full development of liberal institutions. Alternatively, important improvements or

---

3. Dix 1994 (97) and Przeworski and Limongi 1997 (173) date democracy in France to 1875; Stephens (1989) terms 1875–84 a period of consolidation; Vanhanen 1984 (144) states that France crossed the threshold of democracy in the decade of the 1870s; Therborn 1977 dates democracy in France to 1884.

reversals in liberal democracy may take place: "Electoral democracies can become more democratic—more liberal, more constitutional, more competitive, more accountable, more inclusive, and more vigorously participatory," according to Larry Diamond. "They can also become more illiberal, abusive, corrupt, exclusive, narrow, unresponsive and unaccountable—that is, less democratic" (1996, 20). A major question for research is how posttransitional regimes change and whether they will develop fully liberal institutions, for the possibilities are in principle relatively open.

This book considers an important case of a transition to a broad-suffrage electoral regime in which the further development of democratic and liberal institutions was marked by high uncertainty. France in the 1870s was the first country to make a transition to a broad-suffrage electoral democracy in which the full extension of liberal institutions was an open question. Other broad-suffrage countries in the 1870s had previously experienced continuous elite contestation (Switzerland) or were authoritarian (Germany). Seventy years of posttransitional development and a rich historiographical literature make France an ideal case for evaluating hypotheses about development in democracies that cannot yet fully be investigated in the more recent cases. As J. Samuel Valenzuela notes, the "democratic consolidation" in France took decades to complete (1992, 70).

A second broad theme that connects the precursors of the first wave, the first wave, and their third wave counterparts is the range of actors involved in facilitating the transition. Scholars of the third wave emphasize the contributions of both elites and masses in transitions to democracy, although with somewhat more attention to the role of elites (Mainwaring 1992, 302–4). Elites are seen in multiple roles: Divided ruling elites provide critical openings to liberalization (Przeworski 1992); authoritarian elites and leaders of the democratic challenge learn to avoid the recourse to force and choose to permit and participate in opposition politics (Bermeo 1992); elites form pacts, write constitutions, and otherwise "craft" democratic institutions (Karl 1987; Di Palma 1990). On the mass side, however, protest at critical moments can help to bring down an authoritarian regime and mass publics can provide essential pressure for sustained democratization; the common pattern of posttransitional demobilization yields more routine mass participation in democratic institutions (Bova 1992; Bermeo 1987).

At various moments in the development of liberalism, elites and masses played critical roles. One object of this book is to identify the periods in which elites and masses contributed to construction of liberalism of the nineteenth century. Although liberalism was often seen as the project of an exclusive elite, the most successful liberal movements of the nineteenth century also developed mass followings. I argue that in order to build strong liberal movements elites needed to form intraelite ties and new organizations of mass mobilization or else suffer defeat. Elites seeking to establish sustainable regimes were forced to respond to the pressures exerted by the broader society. In addition, successful liberal movements were themselves recast by the experience of leading broad-based organizations.

Scholars of transitions emphasize a wide range of actors that go beyond the categories of elites and masses and some explore the impact of actors in religious organizations. Samuel Huntington places great weight on the role of the Catholic Church in many democratizing episodes:

> In country after country the choice between democracy and authoritarianism became personified in the conflict between the cardinal and the dictator. Catholicism was second only to economic development as a pervasive force making for democratization in the 1970s and 1980s. The logo of the third wave could well be a crucifix superimposed on a dollar sign. (1991, 85)

Before the 1960s the church was usually on good terms with authoritarian regimes and often legitimated them, whereas since then the church has increasingly rejected such positions and has sometimes played a critical role in struggles to remove authoritarian governments (Mainwaring, O'Donnell, and Valenzuela 1992, 7). George Weigel argues that due to their positive experience with democracy U.S. bishops exercised great influence on the Vatican, with their influence culminating in Vatican II's support for liberal principles (1990, 20). This book argues that religion played an equally important role in orienting both elite and mass support for liberalism in the nineteenth century. In particular, the opposition of the Catholic Church to liberalism during the nineteenth century was subject to important national variations and exceptions that go a long way toward explaining the earliest successes of liberal movements.

A third theme concerns the roles of agency and structure in explaining transitions. By focusing on the reaction of liberal elites to religious institutions and the state, I locate the sources of successful liberal transitions as lying between what analysts term economic or social "structure" and political "process" (Karl 1987). "There can be no question that the study of democratic transitions has benefited from the emphasis put on choice," according to Gerardo Munck, "but it is probably also fair to say that the shift from 'prerequisites' to 'process,' or from structural determinants to strategic choices, has gone too far" (1994, 370). Ben Ross Schneider advises that "theory building on democracy . . . may be best advanced by focusing on less aggregate and subregime factors like intermediate organizations, state-society relations, and patterns of representation" (1995, 31). In line with these recommendations, my analysis benefits from the lessons of strategic actor-centered analyses and the perspective of comparative-historical analyses of institutions.

An intermediate position is critical to understanding transitions, for only within the potentially "free zones" of institutional autonomy are resistance and counterorganization possible (Bermeo 1992). What makes a transition possible, according to this line of argument,

> is the prior elaboration, while dictatorship is still in place, of a counterelite anchored in autonomous institutions and buoyed by an alternative political culture. The more articulated and coherent that culture and the institutional frame on which it rests, the more powerful the thrust toward democratization. (Nord 1995b, 9)

Some of the necessary autonomous institutions may be found in firms, business organizations, professional associations, and other institutions located mainly in the economy, as the explanations that focus on socioeconomic development and the middle classes suggest. In the case of nineteenth-century Europe, however, I find that autonomous organizations based in economic relations did not have the capability to carry out a difficult resistance and transition. Rather, I show that there were two types of autonomous institutions critical to liberalism: religious institutions on the one hand and, on the other, organizations that emerged in the conflict between religious institutions and the state.

Liberal institutions are returning to the forefront as scholars attempt to understand the problems of democratic consolidation. The term liberalization in the democratization literature initially focussed attention on one aspect of early liberalism. Guillermo O'Donnell and Philippe C. Schmitter influenced the entire field when they defined liberalization as the initial opening of an authoritarian regime: "the process of making effective certain rights that protect both individuals and social groups from arbitrary or illegal acts committed by the state or third parties" (1986, 7). As scholars come to terms with the complexities and ambiguities of posttransitional politics, they emphasize that liberalism provides the institutional foundation for democratic political order. Liberal institutions are central components of democracies; liberal institutions make the differences between mere electoral regimes on the one hand, and fully liberal democracies on the other. Thus, proceduralist definitions of democracy that require the presence of competition for high office and relatively free and fair elections are supplemented with stringent requirements that civil rights be protected, that governmental actions follow constitutional procedures, and that the state respect freedom of speech, assembly, and association (Collier 1997). Effective freedom of conscience is often not included in the list of rights essential to a fully liberal democracy, but I would argue that it should be included as an essential criterion. These additional criteria that are thought to be essential to a fully democratic system should now be recognizable, in their origins, as the institutions at the heart of liberal party programs: the rule of law, private property, and the distinction between church and state.

Democracies at the end of the twentieth century have some characteristics—and perhaps flaws—that are similar to those of the early nineteenth liberal regimes. Analysts today are concerned about weak political parties (Mainwaring and Scully, 1995) and we have seen that the early liberal regimes emerged prior to the development of strong extraparliamentary parties. The substantial authority exercised by nonelected institutions, such as armies in many new democracies (Agüero 1992), parallels the authority of kings, nonelected upper houses, and armies in the first liberal regimes. Similarly, the systematic social differences in the exercise and effectiveness of political rights in contemporary democratic regimes (Przeworski et al. 1995, 34–39) is not new, but rather a continuation of a problem that liberal regimes have faced since their inception. The tensions between economic liberalism and democratization that analysts identify in recent transitions (Schmitter and Karl 1993, 50–51; Haggard and Kaufman 1992) appear eerily similar to the tensions between economic liberalism and regime change in the nineteenth century. The experience of coalition building that subtended liberal regimes may thus have some implications for crucial attempts to strengthen and deepen the liberal institutions of contemporary regimes.

This study of liberalism advances the ongoing debate regarding the contribution of various social classes to the development of liberal democracy. In my view, the varied success of liberalism in nineteenth- and early twentieth-century Europe cannot be understood without reference to the attempts by liberals to win support from social groups that scholars have previously not emphasized. In a powerful line of argument, leading scholars argue that socioeconomic development and a growing middle class weakened authoritarian landed elites and promoted democracy (Lipset 1959; Moore 1966). A recent rejoinder is that the middle class sometimes pushed for political and civil rights for itself, but only the working class consistently organized for democracy (Rueschemeyer, Stephens, and Stephens 1992). Ruth Collier (1999) responds that the working and middle classes frequently engaged in a joint project to build democracy.

This book shows the importance to liberalism of organizations not covered in these other accounts, namely churches, sects, and religiously oriented political movements. This book also shows the importance to mass-based liberalism and democracy of social classes that are often neglected, but which together made up the majority of European societies—provincial middle classes and peasants. The political construction of class interests implies, in my view, that classes as such do not have predetermined relationships to liberalism and democracy. The political interests of social classes are highly variable; they are pushed in one direction or another by the full array of institutional interests, especially religious institutions, to which they are subject. The findings of this study can thus be seen in the context of a broader reevaluation of how economic development and liberal democracy are connected. In line with the search for a most important cause, Tatu Vanhanen argues that "it is possible to trace the emergence [and survival] of democracy to one regular and dominant causal factor, the relative distribution of power resources, although many other factors may also affect the process of democratization"; the mechanism is that a wide distribution of power resources prevents any single group from exercising hegemony in a political system (1997, 155). Nevertheless, Londregan and Poole find that income has only a modest effect on democracy when they control for historical context (1996, 28). Przeworski and Limongi find that economic development does not provoke transitions to democracy, although economic development does enhance the stability of democratic regimes once they are founded (1997). The critical factor, in my view, in the transitions to liberal regimes and liberal democracies in Europe was thus not economic development alone, but the various political movements mobilized by struggles over the institutional authority of states and churches.

Vibrant communities helped to reinforce and sustain liberal regimes. This book thus argues that liberalism and community are related in complex ways. Communitarian critics of liberalism call for new forms of community and a revived moral center in political life (MacIntyre 1984). Defenders of liberal thought argue, however, that critics of liberalism mischaracterize the liberal vision of society as a mere collection of atomized individuals (Holmes 1993, 190–200). A comparative and historical point of view reveals that religion and liberalism were closely linked, as we are reminded by the religious routes to many examples of European liberalism. In the comparative perspective of this book, we have seen that vibrant communities such as Protestant sects in England, Catholics in Ireland and Belgium, and Protestants in Switzerland all contributed to the creation of liberal institutions. One important path to liberal regimes involved clergy seeking to enhance the authority of religious institutions and defend the civil equality of their members.

In the 1990s, neoliberal economic ideas enjoy an ascendance unmatched since the era of classical liberalism in the middle of the nineteenth century. Privatization of public corporations, market deregulation, global free trade, regional integration, and reductions in some welfare state programs are all hallmarks of the current era (Pierson 1994). Some states are rapidly establishing and enhancing institutions such as independent central banks and international financial institutions that are designed to take the politics out of economic management (Boylan 1998). Neoliberal economic reform can be praised for facilitating economic growth and, at least in the long run, for providing a material basis for democratic politics (Williamson 1994); it can also be criticized for disempowering democratic decision making (Przeworski 1992, 180–91). All of these current developments find parallels in the previous period of "revolutionary expansion" in trade from 1840 to 1914 (Rogowski 1989). Scholars who seek to analyze liberal economic policy and its political implications in the current period will find in the present analysis that the historical context in which political and economic liberalism initially emerged differed substantially from the current period and it remains an open question how liberal institutions will function in the current setting.

In my analysis, I have sought to bring such insights together to argue that liberal societies emerged out of the interplay of increasingly powerful national states, churches, movements for liberal reform, and attempts to define the institutional authority of clergy. The relationships were not universal, but depended on the particular configuration of organizational ties. States that attacked the institutional authority of clergy usually provoked organized movements of religious opposition. Similarly, churches that sought to impose institutional authority over individuals who did not accept clerical direction in a particular realm of life often provoked organized movements to adopt a secularizing agenda. Although not a guarantee of success, liberals could draw strength from the coalitional possibilities inherent in these oppositions. The lessons from the European experience will undoubtedly take distinctive and powerful forms in the political and religious struggles over liberal institutions in the aftermath of democratic transitions around the globe.

Bibliography

Acomb, Evelyn Martha, and Marvin L. Brown, eds. 1966. *French Society and Culture since the Old Regime.* New York: Holt, Reinhart, and Winston.

Agüero, Felipe. 1992. "The Military and the Limits to Democratization in South America." In Scott Mainwaring, Guillermo O'Donnell, and J. Samuel Valenzuela, eds., *Issues in Democratic Consolidation: The New South American Democracies in Comparative Perspective.* Notre Dame, IN: University of Notre Dame Press.

Agulhon, Maurice. 1979 [1970]. *La République au village: Les populations du Var de la révolution à la IIe République.* 2d ed. Paris: Éditions du Seuil.

———. 1993. *The French Republic, 1879–1992.* Cambridge, MA: Blackwell.

Albrecht-Carrié, René. 1977. *Adolphe Thiers, or The Triumph of the Bourgeoisie.* Boston: G. K. Hall.

Allison, John M. S. 1932. *Monsieur Thiers.* London: Allen and Unwin.

Aminzade, Ronald. 1993. *Ballots and Barricades: Class Formation and Republican Politics in France.* Princeton: Princeton University Press.

Anderson, Margaret Lavinia. 1986. "The Kulturkampf and the Course of German History." *Central European History* 19, no. 1 (March): 82–122.

———. 1993. "Voter, Junker, *Landrat,* Priest: The Old Authorities and the New Franchise in Imperial Germany." *American Historical Review* 98, no. 5 (December): 1448–74.

———. 1995. "The Limits of Secularization: On the Problem of the Catholic Revival in Nineteenth-Century Germany." *Historical Journal* 38 (September): 647–70.

Anderson, R. D. 1977. *France 1870–1914, Politics and Society.* London: Routledge and Kegan Paul.

Andrey, Georges. 1983. "Auf der Suche nach dem neuen Staat (1798–1848)." In Comité pour une Nouvelle Histoire de la Suisse, *Geschichte der Schweiz—und der Schweizer.* Vol. 2. Basel: Helbing and Lichtenhahn.

Arblaster, Anthony. 1984. *The Rise and Decline of Western Liberalism.* Oxford: Blackwell.

Artz, Frederick B. 1963 [1934]. *Reaction and Revolution, 1814–1832.* New York: Harper.

Augé-Laribé, Michel. 1940. *La politique agricole de la France de 1880 à 1940.* Paris.

Auspitz, Katherine. 1982. *The Radical Bourgeoisie: The Ligue de l'enseignement and the Origins of the Third Republic, 1866–1885.* Cambridge: Cambridge University Press.

Bairoch, Paul. 1976. "Europe's Gross National Product: 1800–1975." *Journal of European Economic History* 5, no. 2 (fall): 273–340.

———. 1982. "International Industrialization Levels from 1750 to 1980." *Journal of European Economic History* 11, no. 2 (fall): 269–333.
Baker, F. Grenfell. 1895. *The Model Republic: A History of the Rise and Progress of the Swiss People.* London: H. S. Nichols.
Bardonnet, Daniel. 1960. *Évolution de la structure du Parti Radical.* Paris: Éditions Montchrestien.
Barthélemy, Joseph. 1912. *L'Organisation du suffrage et l'expérience belge.* Paris: Giarde et Brière.
Bartier, John. 1981 [1968]. "Partis politiques et classes sociales en Belgique." *Res Publica. Revue de l'Institut belge de science politique* 10: 33–106. Reprinted in John Bartier, *Libéralisme et socialisme au XIXe siècle.* Brussels: Éditions de l'Université de Bruxelles.
Bendix, Reinhard. 1970. "The Age of Ideology: Persistent and Changing." In Reinhard Bendix, *Embattled Reason: Essays on Social Knowledge.* New York: Oxford University Press.
———. 1978. *Kings or People: Power and the Mandate to Rule.* Berkeley: University of California Press.
Bendix, Reinhard, and Stein Rokkan. 1977 [1964]. "The Extension of Citizenship to the Lower Classes." Reprinted in Reinhard Bendix, *Nation-Building and Citizenship.* Berkeley: University of California Press.
Bentley, Michael. 1987. *The Climax of Liberal Politics.* London: Edward Arnold.
Berger, Suzanne. 1982. "Introduction." In Suzanne Berger, ed., *Religion in West European Politics.* London: Cass.
Berg-Schlosser, Dirk, and Gisèle De Meur. 1994. "Conditions of Democracy in Interwar Europe: A Boolean Test of Major Hypotheses." *Comparative Politics* 26, no. 3 (April): 253–79.
Bermeo, Nancy. 1987. "Redemocratization and Transition Elections: A Comparison of Spain and Portugal." *Comparative Politics* 19, no. 2 (January): 213–31.
———. 1992. "Democracy and the Lessons of Dictatorship." *Comparative Politics* 24, no. 3 (April): 273–91.
Berstein, Gisèle, and Serge Berstein. 1987. *La Troisième République.* Paris: M. A. Editions.
Berstein, Serge. 1980. *Histoire du Parti Radical.* Vol. 1. Paris: Presses de la Fondation Nationale des Sciences Politiques.
Biagini, Eugenio F., ed. 1996. *Citizenship and Community: Liberals, Radicals, and Collective Identities in the British Isles, 1865–1931.* Cambridge: Cambridge University Press.
Biaudet, Jean-Charles. 1977. "Der modernen Schweiz entgegen." In *Handbuch der Schweizer Geschichte.* Vol. 2. Zurich: Verlag Berichthaus Zürich.
Bickel, Wilhelm. 1947. *Bevölkerungsgeschichte und Bevölkerungspolitik der Schweiz seit dem Ausgang des Mittelalters.* Habilitationsschrift zur Erlangung der Venia Legendi an der Rechts- und Staatswissenschaftlichen Fakultät der Universität Zürich. Zurich. (Also appears in the series "Forschung und Leben," published by the Büchergilde Gutenberg Zürich.)
Bigler, Robert M. 1972. *The Politics of German Protestantism: The Rise of the Protestant Church Elite in Prussia, 1815–1848.* Berkeley: University of California Press.

Blackbourn, David. 1984. "The Discreet Charm of the Bourgeoisie: Reappraising German History in the Nineteenth Century." In David Blackbourn and Geoff Eley, *The Peculiarities of German History: Bourgeois Society and Politics in Nineteenth-Century Germany.* Oxford: Oxford University Press.

———. 1987. "Progress and Piety: Liberals, Catholics and the State in Bismarck's Germany." In David Blackbourn, *Populists and Patricians: Essays in Modern German History.* London: Allen and Unwin.

———. 1991a. "The German Bourgeoisie: An Introduction." In David Blackbourn and Richard J. Evans, eds., *The German Bourgeoisie: Essays on the Social History of the German Middle Class from the Late Eighteenth to the Early Twentieth Century.* London: Routledge.

———. 1991b. "The Catholic Church in Europe Since the French Revolution" (review). *Comparative Studies in Society and History* 33, no. 4 (October): 778–90.

———. 1994 [1993]. *Marpingen: Apparitions of the Virgin Mary in Nineteenth-Century Germany.* New York: Knopf.

Blackbourn, David, and Geoff Eley. 1984. *The Peculiarities of German History: Bourgeois Society and Politics in Nineteenth-Century Germany.* Oxford: Oxford University Press.

Blackbourn, David, and Richard J. Evans, eds. 1991. *The German Bourgeoisie: Essays on the Social History of the German Middle Class from the Late Eighteenth to the Early Twentieth Century.* London: Routledge.

Bloch, Marc. 1966. *French Rural History: An Essay on its Basic Characteristics.* Trans. Janet Sondheimer. Berkeley: University of California Press.

Bonjour, E., H. S. Offler, and G. R. Potter. 1952. *A Short History of Switzerland.* Oxford: Oxford University Press.

Boutry, Philippe. 1988. "Le mouvement vers Rome et le renouveau missionnaire." In Jacques Le Goff and René Rémond, eds., *Histoire de la France religieuse,* vol. 3. Paris: Seuil.

Bova, Russell. 1992. "Political Dynamics of the Post-Communist Transition: A Comparative Perspective." In Nancy Bermeo, ed., *Liberalization and Democratization: Change in the Soviet Union and Eastern Europe.* Baltimore: Johns Hopkins University Press.

Boylan, Delia. 1998. "Holding Democracy Hostage: Central Bank Autonomy in the Transition From Authoritarian Rule." Paper presented at the fifty-sixth annual meeting of the Midwest Political Science Association, Chicago, April.

Bressolette, Claude. 1984. *Le pouvoir dans la société et dans l'Église.* Paris: Les Éditions du Cerf.

Breuilly, John. 1992. *Labour and Liberalism in Nineteenth-Century Europe: Essays in Comparative History.* Manchester: Manchester University Press.

Brogan, Denis. 1940. *The Development of Modern France.* London: Hamish Hamilton.

Callier, Albert. 1878. "L'Élection du 11 juin 1878." *Revue de Belgique,* 15 Juillet. Brussels: Muquardt.

Carte figurative des élections communales du 19 octobre 1884 dressée en réponse à la Carte de Monsieur J. Malou. January 1885. Archives Générales du Royaume, Brussels, Belgium.

Casanova, José. 1994. *Public Religions in the Modern World.* Chicago: University of Chicago Press.
Chaves, Mark. 1994. "Secularization as Declining Religious Authority." *Social Forces* 72 (March): 749–74.
Childers, Thomas. 1983. *The Nazi Voter: The Social Foundations of Fascism in Germany, 1919–1933.* Chapel Hill: University of North Carolina Press.
Christophe, Robert. 1966. *Le siècle de Monsieur Theirs.* Paris: Librarie Académique Perrin.
Clough, Shepard Bancroft, and Charles Woolsey Cole. 1952. *Economic History of Europe.* 3d ed. Boston: D. C. Heath.
Cobban, Alfred. 1981 [1957]. *A History of Modern France.* 3 vols. London: Penguin.
Collier, David. 1997. "Democracy with Adjectives: Conceptual Innovation in Comparative Research." *World Politics* 49, no. 3 (April): 430–51.
Collier, Ruth Berins. 1999. *Paths toward Democracy: The Working Class and Elites in Western Europe and South America.* Cambridge: Cambridge University Press.
Collier, Ruth Berins, and David Collier. 1991. *Shaping the Political Arena: Critical Junctures, the Labor Movement, and Regime Dynamics in Latin America.* Princeton: Princeton University Press.
Collingham, H. A. C. 1988. *The July Monarchy: A Political History of France, 1830–1848.* London: Longman.
Comité pour une Nouvelle Histoire de la Suisse. 1983. *Geschichte der Schweiz—und der Schweizer.* Vol. 2. Basel: Helbing and Lichtenhahn.
Congrès Libéral de Belgique. 1846. "Programme du libéralisme," procès-verbal de la séance du 14 juin. Proceedings of the Liberal Congress may be found in the Fonds Stevens II 4742 A v. 28 of the Bibliothèque Générale du Royaume de Belgique and the Fonds Frère-Orban no. 164 of the Archives Générales.
Conrad, Carl-August. 1970. *Die politischen Parteien im Verfassungssystem der Schweiz.* Frankfurt: Athanäum.
Craig, Gordon A. 1988. *The Triumph of Liberalism: Zürich in the Golden Age, 1830–1869.* New York: Scribner's.
Dahl, Robert A., ed. 1966. *Political Oppositions in Western Democracies.* New Haven: Yale University Press.
———. 1971. *Polyarchy: Participation and Opposition.* New Haven: Yale University Press.
Dahrendorf, Ralf. 1979 [1967]. *Society and Democracy in Germany.* New York: W. W. Norton.
Dändliker, Karl. 1899. *A Short History of Switzerland.* London: Swan Sonnenschein; New York: Macmillan.
Dansette, Adrien. 1961 [1948]. *Religious History of Modern France.* Trans. John Dingle. Freiburg: Herder.
Delange-Janson, Léon. 1962. *Paul Janson, 1840–1913.* 2 vols. Brussels: Éditions du Centre Paul Hymans.
De Meur, Gisèle, and Dirk Berg-Schlosser. 1996. "Conditions of Authoritarianism, Fascism, and Democracy in Interwar Europe: Systematic Matching and Contrasting of Cases for 'Small N' Analysis." *Comparative Political Studies* 29, no. 4 (August): 423–68.

De Ruggiero, Guido. 1959 [1927]. *The History of European Liberalism.* Trans. R. G. Collingwood. Boston: Beacon Press.
De Schweinitz, Karl. 1964. *Industrialization and Democracy.* New York: Free Press.
Diamond, Larry. 1992. "Economic Development and Democracy Reconsidered." *American Behavioral Scientist* 35, no. 4/5 (March/June): 450–99.
———. 1996. "Is the Third Wave Over?" *Journal of Democracy* 7, no. 3 (July): 20–37.
Diefendorf, J. M. 1980. *Businessmen and Politics in the Rhineland, 1789–1834.* Princeton: Princeton University Press.
Di Palma, Giuseppe. 1990. *To Craft Democracies: An Essay on Democratic Transitions.* Berkeley: University of California Press.
Di Stefano, Christine. 1991. *Configurations of Masculinity: A Feminist Perspective on Modern Political Theory.* Ithaca: Cornell University Press.
Le Dix Juin, ses auteurs, ses causes et ses suites: quelques réflexions à propos des derniers événements politiques en Belgique. 1884. Brussels: Librarie polytechnique, Jules Decq. Located in the Archives Générales du Royaume de Belgique, Fonds Frère-Orban no. 166. (This anonymous brochure was penned by Mathieu Jacquinet, according to the *Bibliographie Nationale.*)
Dix, Robert H. 1994. "History and Democracy Revisited." *Comparative Politics* 27, no. 1 (October): 91–105.
Downing, Brian. 1992. *The Military Revolution and Political Change: Origins of Democracy and Autocracy in Early Modern Europe.* Princeton: Princeton University Press.
Droz, Jacques. 1966. "Religious Aspects of the Revolutions of 1848 in Europe." In Evelyn M. Acomb and Marvin L. Brown, eds., *French Society and Culture Since the Old Regime.* New York: Holt, Rinehart and Winston.
Dunn, John. 1992. "Conclusion." In John Dunn, ed., *Democracy: The Unfinished Journey, 508 BC to AD 1993.* Oxford: Oxford University Press.
L'Echo du Parlement. April 28, 1882. Brussels.
Eley, Geoff. 1984. "The British Model and the German Road: Rethinking the Course of German History Before 1914." In David Blackbourn and Geoff Eley, *The Peculiarities of German History: Bourgeois Society and Politics in Nineteenth-Century Germany.* Oxford: Oxford University Press.
———. 1991. "Liberalism, Europe, and the Bourgeoisie: 1860–1914." In David Blackbourn and Richard J. Evans, eds., *The German Bourgeoisie: Essays on the Social History of the German Middle Class from the Late Eighteenth to the Early Twentieth Century.* London: Routledge.
Ellens, J. P. 1994. *Religious Routes to Gladstonian Liberalism: The Church Rate Conflict in England and Wales, 1832–1868.* University Park: Pennsylvania State University Press.
Elwitt, Sanford. 1975. *The Making of the Third Republic: Class and Politics in France, 1868–1884.* Baton Rouge: Louisiana State University Press.
Ertman, Thomas. 1997. *Birth of the Leviathan: Building States and Regimes in Medieval and Early Modern Europe.* Cambridge: Cambridge University Press.
Evans, Richard J. 1987. *Rethinking German History: Nineteenth-Century Germany and the Origins of the Third Reich.* London: Unwin Hyman.
Evans, Richard J., and W. R. Lee., eds. 1986. *The German Peasantry: Conflict and*

138   Bibliography

Community in Rural Society from the Eighteenth to the Twentieth Centuries. London: Croom Helm.

Eyck, Frank. 1968. *The Frankfurt Parliament, 1848–1849.* London: Macmillan.

———. 1983. "Liberalismus und Katholizismus in der Zeit des deutschen Vormärz." In Wolfgang Schieder, ed., *Liberalismus in der Gesellschaft des deutschen Vormärz.* Göttingen: Vandenhoeck und Ruprecht.

Farmer, Paul. 1971 [1960]. "The Second Empire in France." In *The New Cambridge Modern History.* Vol. 10. Cambridge: Cambridge University Press.

Farr, Ian. 1986. "'Tradition' and the Peasantry: On the Modern Historiography of Rural Germany." In Richard J. Evans and W. R. Lee, eds., *The German Peasantry: Conflict and Community in Rural Society from the Eighteenth to the Twentieth Centuries.* London: Croom Helm.

Fehrenbach, Elisabeth. 1983. "Rheinischer Liberalismus und gesellschaftliche Verfassung." In Wolfgang Schieder, ed., *Liberalismus in der Gesellschaft des deutschen Vormärz.* Göttingen: Vandenhoeck und Ruprecht.

(La) Feuille du Village. 1849–51. Journal politique hebdomadaire.

Fischer, Wolfram, ed. 1985. *Handbuch der europäischen Wirtschafts- und Sozialgeschichte.* Vol. 5, *Europäischen Wirtschafts- und Sozialgeschichte von der Mitte des 19. Jahrhunderts bis zum ersten Weltkrieg.* Stuttgart: Klett-Cotta.

Fishman, Robert, 1990. "Rethinking State and Regime: Southern Europe's Transition to Democracy." *World Politics* 42, no. 3 (April): 422–40.

Flamant, Maurice. 1988. *Histoire du libéralisme.* Series: "Que sais-je?" Paris: Presses Universitaires de France.

Flora, Peter. 1983a. "Stein Rokkan's Macro-Modell of Europe." In Peter Flora, ed., *State, Economy, and Society in Western Europe 1815–1975: A Data Handbook,* 1:1–26.

———. ed. 1983b. *State, Economy, and Society in Western Europe 1815–1975: A Data Handbook,* vol. 1. Frankfurt: Campus Verlag; London: Macmillan; Chicago: St. James.

Flora, Peter, and Jens Alber. 1987. *State, Economy, and Society in Western Europe 1815–1975: A Data Handbook,* vol. 2. Frankfurt: Campus Verlag; London: Macmillan; Chicago: St. James.

Frère-Orban, Walther. 1879. *Discours* prononcé par M. Frère-Orban, séance du 27 mai 1879 dans la Chambre des Représentants pendant la discussion du projet de loi portant révision de la loi de 1842 sur l'enseignement primaire. Brussels: Hayez.

Fulbrook, Mary. 1983. *Piety and Politics: Religion and the Rise of Absolutism in England, Württemberg, and Prussia.* Cambridge: Cambridge University Press.

Furet, François. 1992. *Revolutionary France, 1770–1880.* Trans. Antonia Nevill. Oxford: Blackwell.

Gerschenkron, Alexander. 1962. *Economic Backwardness in Historical Perspective: A Book of Essays.* Cambridge: Harvard University Press.

Gildea, Robert. 1983. *Education in Provincial France, 1800–1914.* London: Oxford University Press.

Gilliard, Charles. 1955. *A History of Switzerland.* Trans. D. L. B. Hartley. London: Allen and Unwin.

Girard, Louis. 1966. "Political Liberalism in France, 1840–1875." Trans. Joseph N.

Moody. In Evelyn Martha Acomb and Marvin L. Brown, eds., *French Society and Culture since the Old Regime*. New York: Holt, Reinhart and Winston.
———. 1967. *Le Libéralisme en France de 1814 à 1848, doctrine et mouvements*. Paris: Éditions du Seuil.
———. 1985. *Les libéraux français, 1814–1875*. Paris: Aubier.
Golob, Eugene O. 1944. *The Méline Tariff: French Agriculture and Nationalist Economic Policy*. New York: Columbia University Press.
Gossman, Lionel. 1994. "Basel." In Nicolas Bouvier, Gordon A. Craig, and Gossman, *Geneva, Zurich, Basel: History, Culture, and National Identity*. Princeton: Princeton University Press.
Goualt, Jacques. 1954. *Comment la France est devenue républicaine*. Series: Cahiers de la fondation nationale des sciences politiques (62). Paris: Librarie Armand Colin.
Gougel, François. 1958 [1946]. *La politique des parties sous la IIIe république*. 3d ed. Paris.
Gourevitch, Peter. 1986. *Politics in Hard Times: Comparative Responses to International Economic Crises*. Ithaca: Cornell University Press.
Gruner, Erich. 1943. *Das bernische Patriziat und die Regeneration*. Inaugural-Dissertation der philosophischen Fakultät der Universität Bern zur Erlangung der Doktorwürde. Bern: Buchdruckerei Feuz. (Also appears in *Archiv des Historischen Vereins des Kantons Bern* 37 (1943).)
———. 1978. *Die Wahlen in den Schweizerischen Nationalrat, 1848–1919*. 3 vols. Bern: Francke Verlag.
Gruner, Erich, and Karl Frei. 1966. *Die Schweizerische Bundesversammlung, 1848–1920*. Vol. 2, *Soziologie und Statistik*. Bern: Francke Verlag.
Gubin, Eliane, and Patrick Lefèvre. 1985. "Obligation scolaire et société en Belgique au XIXe siècle." *Revue Belge de Philologie et d'Histoire* 63, in two parts, nos. 2 and 4.
Guillaume, Pierre. 1984. "Les libéraux français, 1848–1870." In Pierre Guillaume, ed., *Diversité du libéralisme politique en Europe au XIXe siècle*. Travaux de la Maison des Sciences de l'Homme d'Aquitaine, no. 2. Paris: Economica.
Guillaume, Pierre, ed. 1984. *Diversité du libéralisme politique en Europe au XIXe siècle*. Travaux de la Maison des Sciences de l'homme d'Aquitaine, no. 2. Paris: Economica.
Guiral, Pierre. 1986. *Adolphe Thiers, ou De la nécessité en politique*. Paris: Librairie Arthème Fayard.
Haggard, Stephan, and Robert R. Kaufman. 1992. "Economic Adjustment and the Prospects of Democracy." In Stephan Haggard and Robert R. Kaufman, eds., *The Politics of Economic Adjustment: International Constraints, Distributive Conflicts, and the State*. Princeton: Princeton University Press.
Hall, John A. 1987. *Liberalism: Politics, Ideology and the Market*. Chapel Hill: University of North Carolina Press.
Hall, Peter A. 1986. *Governing the Economy: The Politics of State Intervention in Britain and France*. New York: Oxford University Press.
Hamerow, Theodore S. 1969. *The Social Foundations of German Unification, 1858–1871: Ideas and Institutions*. Princeton: Princeton University Press.
Hause, Steven C., with Anne R. Kenney. 1984. *Women's Suffrage and Social Politics in the French Third Republic*. Princeton: Princeton University Press.

Hilaire, Yves-Marie, André Legrand, Bernard Ménager and Robert Vandenbussche, eds. 1977. *Atlas électoral Nord, Pas-de-Calais, 1876–1936.* Villeneuve-d'Ascq: Publications de l'Université de Lille III.

Hill, Keith. 1974. "Belgium: Political Change in a Segmented Society." In Richard Rose, ed., *Electoral Behavior: A Comparative Handbook.* New York: Free Press.

Hoffmann, Stanley. 1963. "Paradoxes of the French Political Community." In Stanley Hoffmann, ed., *In Search of France.* Cambridge: Harvard University Press.

Höhne, Roland, and Ingo Kolboom. 1987. "Aufsteig, Niedergang und Renaissance des Liberalismus in Frankreich." In Hans Vorländer, ed., *Verfall oder Renaissance des Liberalismus?* Munich: Günter Olzog Verlag.

Holborn, Hajo. 1969. *A History of Modern Germany.* 3 vols. New York: Knopf.

Holden, Catherine M. 1954. "A Decade of Dissent in Germany: An Historical Study of the Society of Protestant Friends and the German-Catholic Church, 1840–1848." Ph.D. diss., Department of History, Yale University.

Holmes, Stephen. 1984. *Benjamin Constant and the Making of Modern Liberalism.* New Haven: Yale University Press.

———. 1993. *The Anatomy of Antiliberalism.* Cambridge, MA: Harvard University Press.

Horvath-Peterson, Sandra. 1991. "Introduction" to the Forum on the Third Republic in *French Historical Studies* 17, no. 2 (fall): 302–3.

Huard, Raymond. 1985. "Comment apprivoiser le suffrage universel?" In Daniel Gaxie, ed., *Explication du vote: un bilan des études électorales en France.* Paris: Presses de la Fondation Nationale des Sciences Politiques.

Huntington, Samuel. 1991. *The Third Wave: Democratization in the Late Twentieth Century.* Norman: University of Oklahoma Press.

———. 1996. *The Clash of Civilizations and the Remaking of World Order.* New York: Simon and Schuster.

Huyse, Luc. 1981. "Political Conflict in Bicultural Belgium." In Arend Lijphart, ed., *Conflict and Coexistence in Belgium: The Dynamics of a Culturally Divided Society.* Research Series 46. Berkeley: Institute of International Studies, University of California.

L'Illustration, journal universel. 1846. Vol. 7, no. 175.

Inglehart, Margaret. 1979. "Sex Role, Historical Heritage, and Political Participation in Switzerland. In Howard R. Penniman, ed., *Switzerland at the Polls: The National Elections of 1979.* Washington, DC: American Enterprise Institute for Public Policy Research.

Inglehart, Ronald. 1977. *The Silent Revolution: Changing Values and Political Styles Among Western Publics.* Princeton: Princeton University Press.

———. 1990. *Culture Shift in Advanced Industrial Society.* Princeton: Princeton University Press.

Isoart, Paul, and Christian Bidegaray, eds. 1988. *Des Républiques françaises.* Paris: Économica.

Janos, Andrew C. 1989. "The Politics of Backwardness in Continental Europe, 1780–1945." *World Politics* 61, no. 3 (April): 325–58.

Jarausch, Konrad H., and Larry Eugene Jones. 1990. "German Liberalism Reconsidered: Inevitable Decline, Bourgeois Hegemony, or Partial Achievement?" In Konrad H. Jarausch and Larry Eugene Jones, eds., *In Search of a Liberal Germany: Studies in the History of German Liberalism from 1789 to the Present.* New York: Berg.

Jardin, André. 1985. *Histoire du libéralisme politique, de la crise de l'absolutisme à la constitution de 1875.* Paris: Hachette.

———. 1988. *Tocqueville: A Biography.* Trans. by Lydia Davis with Robert Hemenway. New York: Farrar Straus Giroux.

Jenkins, T. A. 1988. *Gladstone, Whiggery and the Liberal Party 1874–1886.* Oxford: Oxford University Press.

Johnson, Douglas. 1963. *Guizot: Aspects of French History, 1787–1874.* London: Routledge and Kegan Paul.

Jones, P. M. 1985. *Politics and Rural Society: The Southern Massif Central, c. 1750–1880.* Cambridge: Cambridge University Press.

Junker, Beat. 1990. *Geschichte des Kantons Bern seit 1798,* Vol. 2, *Die Entstehung des demokratischen Volksstaates, 1831–1880.* Bern: Archiv des Historischen Vereins des Kantons Bern.

Kalyvas, Stathis. 1996. *The Rise of Christian Democracy.* Ithaca: Cornell University Press.

Karl, Terry Lynn. 1987. "Petroleum and Political Pacts: The Transition to Democracy in Venezuela." *Latin American Research Review* 22, no. 1: 63–94.

Katzenstein, Peter J. 1984. *Corporatism and Change: Austria, Switzerland, and the Politics of Industry.* Ithaca: Cornell University Press.

———. 1985. *Small States in World Markets: Industrial Policy in Europe.* Ithaca: Cornell University Press.

Kayser, Jacques. 1962. *Les grandes batailles du radicalisme des origines aux portes du pouvoir, 1820–1901.* Paris: Rivière.

Kirchner, Emil J., ed. 1988. *Liberal Parties in Western Europe.* Cambridge: Cambridge University Press.

Kitschelt, Herbert. 1992. Review Article. *American Political Science Review* 86, no. 4 (December): 1028–34.

Kocka, Jürgen. 1993. "The European Pattern and the German Case." In Jürgen Kocka and Allan Mitchell, eds., *Bourgeois Society in Nineteenth-Century Europe.* Oxford: Berg.

Kocka, Jürgen, ed. 1986. *Arbeiter und Bürger im 19. Jahrhundert. Varianten ihres Verhältnisses im europäischen Vergleich.* Munich: R. Oldenbourg.

Kocka, Jürgen, and Ute Frevert, eds. 1988. *Das Bürgertum im 19. Jahrhundert. Deutschland im europäischen Vergleich.* Munich: DTV.

Kocka, Jürgen, and Allan Mitchell, eds. 1993. *Bourgeois Society in Nineteenth-Century Europe.* Oxford: Berg. (Translated selections from Kocka and Frevert 1988.)

Kossmann, E. H. 1978. *The Low Countries, 1780–1940.* Oxford: Clarendon.

Krieger, Leonard. 1972 [1957]. *The German Idea of Freedom. History of a Political Tradition.* Chicago: University of Chicago Press.

Kurth, James. 1979. "Industrial Change and Political Change: A European Perspective." In David Collier, ed., *The New Authoritarianism in Latin America.* Princeton: Princeton University Press.

Laboulaye, Édouard. 1851. *La révision de la Constitution: Lettres à un ami.* Paris: Durand.

Lagoueyte, Patrick. 1989. *La vie politique en France au xixe siècle.* Paris: Ophrys.

Langewiesche, Dieter. 1983. "Gesellschafts- und verfassungpolitische Handlungsbedingungen und Zielvorstellungen europäischer Liberaler in den Revolutionen von 1848." In Wolfgang Schieder, ed., *Liberalismus in der Gesellschaft des deutschen Vormärz.* Göttingen: Vandenhoeck und Ruprecht.

———. 1988a. *Liberalismus in Deutschland.* Frankfurt: Suhrkamp.

———. 1988b. "Deutscher Liberalismus im europäischen Vergleich. Konzeption und Ergebnisse." In Dieter Langewiesche, ed., *Liberalismus im 19. Jahrhundert: Deutschland im europäischen Vergleich.* Göttingen: Vandenhoeck und Ruprecht.

———. 1990. "German Liberalism in the Second Empire, 1871–1914." In Konrad H. Jarausch and Larry Eugene Jones, eds., *In Search of a Liberal Germany: Studies in the History of German Liberalism from 1789 to the Present.* New York: Berg.

———. 1993. "Liberalism and the Middle Classes in Europe." In Jürgen Kocka and Allan Mitchell, eds. *Bourgeois Society in Nineteenth-Century Europe.*

LaPalombara, Joseph, and Myron Weiner, eds. 1964. *Political Parties and Political Development.* Princeton: Princeton University Press.

Laski, Harold J. 1958 [1936]. *The Rise of European Liberalism: An Essay in Interpretation.* London: Allen and Unwin.

Laurent, F. 1878. "La Loi de 1842." *Revue de Belgique,* 15 Novembre. Brussels: Muquardt.

Lebovics, Herman. 1988. *The Alliance of Iron and Wheat in the Third French Republic, 1860–1914. Origins of a New Conservatism.* Baton Rouge: Louisiana State University Press.

Lefèvre, Patrick. 1989. "L'Organisation du parti libéral de 1846 à 1914." In Hervé Hasquin and Adriaan Verhulst, eds., *Le Libéralisme en Belgique: Deux cents ans d'histoire.* Brussels: Centre Paul Hymans, Editions Delta.

Lenger, Friedrich. 1990. "Bürgertum und Stadtverwaltung in rheinischen Grossstädten des 19. Jahrhunderts: zu einem vernachlässigten Aspekt bürgerlicher Herrschaft." In Lothar Gall, ed., *Stadt und Bürgertum im 19. Jahrhundert.* Munich: R. Oldenbourg Verlag.

Lenman, Robin. 1981. Review. *English Historical Review* 96 (July): 660–61.

Lichbach, Mark Irving. 1996. *The Cooperator's Dilemma.* Ann Arbor: University of Michigan Press.

Lijphart, Arend. 1977. *Democracy in Plural Societies: A Comparative Explanation.* New Haven: Yale University Press.

———. 1981. "Introduction: The Belgian Example of Cultural Coexistence in Comparative Perspective." In Arend Lijphart, ed., *Conflict and Coexistence in Belgium: The Dynamics of a Culturally Divided Society.* Research Series 46. Berkeley: Institute of International Studies, University of California.

———. 1984. *Democracies: Patterns of Majoritarian and Consensus Government in Twenty-One Countries.* New Haven: Yale University Press.

Linz, Juan, and Arturo Valenzuela, eds. 1994. *The Failure of Presidential Democracy.* Baltimore: Johns Hopkins University Press.

Lipset, Seymour Martin. 1981 [1959]. *Political Man: The Social Bases of Politics.* Baltimore: Johns Hopkins University Press.

———. 1968. *Revolution and Counterrevolution: Change and Persistence in Social Structures.* New York: Basic.

———. 1983. "Radicalism or Reformism: The Sources of Working-class Politics." *American Political Science Review* 77, no. 1 (March): 1–18.

Lipset, Seymour Martin, and Stein Rokkan. 1967. "Cleavage Structures, Party Systems and Voter Alignments: An Introduction." In Seymour Martin Lipset and Stein Rokkan, eds., *Party Systems and Voter Alignments: Cross-National Perspectives.* New York: Free Press.

Locke, Richard, and Kathleen Thelen. 1995. "Apples and Oranges Revisited: Contextualized Comparisons and the Study of Comparative Labor Politics." *Politics and Society* 23, no. 3 (September): 337–67.

Londregan, John B., and Keith T. Poole. 1996. "Does High Income Promote Democracy?" *World Politics* 49, no. 1 (October): 1–30.

Lorwin, Val. 1966. "Belgium." In Robert A. Dahl, ed., *Political Oppositions in Western Democracies.* New Haven: Yale University Press.

———. 1971. "Segmented Pluralism: Ideological Cleavages and Political Cohesion in the Smaller European Democracies." *Comparative Politics* 3, no. 2 (January): 217–49.

Luebbert, Gregory M. 1987. "Origins of Inter-war Regimes in Europe." *World Politics* 34 (July): 449–78.

———. 1991. *Liberalism, Fascism, or Social Democracy: Social Classes and the Political Origins of Regimes in Interwar Europe.* New York: Oxford University Press.

Machin, G. I. T. 1977. *Politics and the Churches in Great Britain, 1832 to 1868.* Oxford: Oxford University Press.

———. 1987. *Politics and the Churches in Great Britain, 1869 to 1921.* Oxford: Clarendon Press.

MacIntyre, Alasdair. 1984. *After Virtue: A Study in Moral Theory.* 2d ed. Notre Dame, IN: University of Notre Dame Press.

Mackie, Thomas T., and Richard Rose. 1991. *The International Almanac of Electoral History.* 3d ed. Washington, DC: Congressional Quarterly.

Maddison, Angus. 1995. *Monitoring the World Economy: 1820–1992.* Development Centre of the Organisation for Economic Co-operation and Development.

Madeley, John. 1982. "Politics and the Pulpit: The Case of Protestant Europe." In Suzanne Berger, ed., *Religion in West European Politics.* London: Cass.

Magraw, Roger. 1986 [1983]. *France, 1815–1914: The Bourgeois Century.* London: Oxford University Press.

———. 1992. *A History of the French Working Class.* 2 vols. Oxford: Blackwell.

Maier, Charles S. 1987. *In Search of Stability: Explorations in Historical Political Economy.* Cambridge: Cambridge University Press.

Mainwaring, Scott. 1992. "Transitions to Democracy and Democratic Consolidation: Theoretical and Comparative Issues." In Scott Mainwaring, Guillermo O'Donnell, and J. Samuel Valenzuela, eds., *Issues in Democratic Consolidation: The New*

South American Democracies in Comparative Perspective, 294–342. Notre Dame, IN: University of Notre Dame Press.

Mainwaring, Scott, Guillermo O'Donnell, and J. Samuel Valenzuela. 1992. "Introduction." In Scott Mainwaring, Guillermo O'Donnell, and J. Samuel Valenzuela, eds., *Issues in Democratic Consolidation: The New South American Democracies in Comparative Perspective.* Notre Dame, IN: University of Notre Dame Press.

Mainwaring, Scott, and Timothy Scully, eds. 1995. *Building Democratic Institutions: Party Systems in Latin America.* Stanford: Stanford University Press.

Mainwaring, Scott, and Matthew Shugart. 1993. "Juan Linz, Presidentialism, and Democracy: A Critical Appraisal." Working Paper No. 200. Notre Dame, IN: The Helen Kellogg Institute for International Studies.

Malou, Jules. [1884]. *Carte figurative.* Archives Générales du Royaume, Brussels.

Manent, Pierre. 1994. *An Intellectual History of Liberalism.* Translated by Rebecca Balinski. Princeton: Princeton University Press.

Margadant, T. W. 1979. *French Peasants in Revolt: The Insurrection of 1851.* Princeton: Princeton University Press.

Marshall, T. H. 1964. *Class, Citizenship and Social Development.* Garden City, NY: Doubleday.

Martin, David. 1978. *A General Theory of Secularization.* Oxford: Blackwell.

Martin, William. 1971. *Switzerland from Roman Times to the Present.* Trans. Jocasta Innes. Originally published as *Histoire de la Suisse.* New York: Praeger.

Marx, Karl. 1977 [1852]. *The Eighteenth Brumaire of Louis Bonaparte.* New York: International Publishers.

Mayeur, Jean-Marie. 1968. *Un prêtre démocrate, l'abbé Lemire (1853–1928).* Paris: Casterman.

———. 1984. *La vie politique sous la troisième République, 1870–1940.* Paris: Éditions du Seuil.

McCarthy, John D., and Meyer N. Zald. 1977. "Resource Mobilization and Social Movements: A Partial Theory." *American Journal of Sociology* 82:1217–18.

McPhee, Peter. 1992. *The Politics of Rural Life: Political Mobilization in the French Countryside, 1846–1852.* Oxford: Oxford University Press.

Ménager, Bernard. 1983 [1979]. *La vie politique dans le département du Nord de 1851 à 1877.* 3 vols. Thèse présentée devant l'Université de Paris IV, le 14 juin 1979. Lille: Atèlier National Réproduction des Theses, Université Lille III; Dunkerque: Diffusion Les Éditions des Beffrois.

Merriman, John. 1978. *The Agony of the Republic: The Repression of the Left in Revolutionary France, 1848–1851.* New Haven and London: Yale University Press.

———. 1985. *The Red City: Limoges and the French Nineteenth Century.* New York: Oxford University Press.

Milward, Alan S. 1990. Review article. *Journal of Modern History* 62, no. 1 (March): 105–8.

Milward, Alan S., and S. B. Saul. 1973. *The Economic Development of Continental Europe, 1780–1870.* Vol. 1. London: Allen and Unwin.

Moody, Joseph N. 1966. "French Liberal Catholics, 1840–1875." In Evelyn M. Acomb and Marvin L. Brown, Jr., eds., *French Society and Culture Since the Old Regime.* New York: Holt, Rinehart and Winston.

Moore, Barrington. 1966. *Social Origins of Dictatorship and Democracy: Lord and Peasant in the Making of the Modern World.* Boston: Beacon Press.

Moses, Claire Goldberg, and Leslie Wahl Rabine. 1993. *Feminism, Socialism, and French Romanticism.* Bloomington: Indiana University Press.

Munck, Gerardo L. 1994. "Democratic Transitions in Comparative Perspective." *Comparative Politics* 26, no. 3 (April): 355–75.

Nipperdey, Thomas. 1961. *Die Organisation der deutschen Parteien vor 1918.* Düsseldorf: Droste Verlag.

Nord, Philip. 1995a. "The Origins of the Third Republic in France, 1860–1885." In George Reid Andrews and Herrick Chapman, eds., *The Social Construction of Democracy.* New York: New York University Press.

———. 1995b. *The Republican Moment: Struggles for Democracy in Nineteenth Century France.* Cambridge, MA: Harvard University Press.

O'Donnell, Guillermo. 1979. "Notas para el estudio de procesos de democratización política a partir del estado burocrático-autoritário." Estudios CEDES 2, no. 5.

———. 1996. "Another Institutionalization: Latin America and Elsewhere." *Journal of Democracy* 7, no. 2 (April).

O'Donnell, Guillermo, and Philippe C. Schmitter. 1986. *Tentative Conclusions About Uncertain Democracies.* Baltimore: Johns Hopkins University Press.

Ostrom, Elinor. 1991. "Rational Choice Theory and Institutional Analysis: Toward Complementarity" [Review]. *American Political Science Review* 85, no. 1 (March): 237–43.

Parry, Jonathan. 1986. *Democracy and Religion: Gladstone and the Liberal Party, 1867–1875.* Cambridge: Cambridge Unversity Press.

———. 1993. *The Rise and Fall of Liberal Government in Victorian Britain.* New Haven: Yale University Press.

Paxton, Robert O. 1982 [1972]. *Vichy France: Old Guard and New Order, 1940–1944.* 2d ed. New York: Columbia University.

Pflanze, Otto. 1990 [1963]. *Bismarck and the Development of Germany.* 3 vols. [previously published as one]. Princeton: Princeton University Press.

Pierson, Paul. 1994. *Dismantling the Welfare State? Reagan, Thatcher and the Politics of Retrenchment.* New York: Cambridge University Press.

Pilbeam, Pamela M. 1990. *The Middle Classes in Europe, 1789–1914: France, Germany, Italy and Russia.* Chicago: Lyceum.

Poggi, Gianfranco. 1978. *The Development of the Modern State: A Sociological Introduction.* Stanford: Stanford University Press.

Pounds, N. J. G. 1990. *An Historical Geography of Europe.* Cambridge: Cambridge University Press.

Le Précuseur. March 30, 1882. Brussels.

Programmes, professions de Foi et engagements électoraux de 1881. Tome 2, no. 808 (Annexes) Chambre des Députés, Troisième Législature, session de 1882. Annexes au procès-verbal de la séance du 9 mai, 1882. Paris.

Przeworski, Adam. 1991. *Democracy and the Market.* Cambridge: Cambridge University Press.

———. 1992. "The Games of Transition." In Scott Mainwaring, Guillermo O'Donnell, and J. Samuel Valenzuela, eds., *Issues in Democratic Consolidation: The New*

South American Democracies in Comparative Perspective. Notre Dame, IN: University of Nortre Dame Press.

Przeworski, Adam, Michael Alvarez, José Antonio Cheibub, and Fernando Limongi. 1996. "What Makes Democracies Endure?" *Journal of Democracy* 7, no. 1 (January): 39–55.

Przeworski, Adam, et al. 1995. *Sustainable Democracy.* Cambridge: Cambridge University Press.

Przeworski, Adam, and Fernando Limongi. 1997. "Modernization: Theories and Facts." *World Politics* 49, no. 2 (January): 155–83.

Puissant, Jean. 1982. *L'Evolution du mouvement ouvrier socialiste dans le Borinage.* Brussels.

Reardon, Bernard M. G. 1975. *Liberalism and Tradition.* Cambridge: Cambridge University Press.

Remmer, Karen. 1995. "New Theoretical Perspectives on Democratization" (review). *Comparative Politics* 28, no. 1 (October): 103–22.

Rémond, René. 1969 [1963]. *The Right Wing in France: From 1815 to de Gaulle.* 2nd American edition. Translated by James M. Laux. Philadelphia: University of Pennsylvania Press.

———. 1976. *L'Anticléricalisme en France, de 1815 à nos jours.* Paris: Fayard.

Revue de Belgique. Various dates. Brussels: Muquardt.

Rogowski, Ronald. 1989. *Commerce and Coalitions: How Trade Affects Domestic Political Alignments.* Princeton: Princeton University Press.

Rohe, Karl. 1986. *Vom Revier zum Ruhrgebiet.* Essen: Reimar Hobbing.

Rose, Richard, and Derek Urwin. 1969. "Social Cohesion, Political Parties and Strains in Regimes." *Comparative Political Studies* 2:7–67.

———. 1970. "Persistence and Change in Western Party Systems Since 1945." *Political Studies* 18:287–319.

Rosenberg, Hans. 1933. *Rudolf Haym und die Anfänge des Klassischen Liberalismus.* Munich and Berlin: R. Oldenbourg.

Ross, Ronald J. 1982. Review. *American Historical Review* 87 (October): 1118.

Rueschemeyer, Dietrich, Evelyne Huber Stephens, and John D. Stephens. 1992. *Capitalist Development and Democracy.* Chicago: University of Chicago Press.

Ruffieux, Roland. 1983. "Die Schweiz des Freisinns (1848–1914)." In Comité pour une Nouvell Histoire de la Suisse, *Geschichte der Schweiz—und der Schweizer.* Vol. 3. Basel: Helbing and Lichtenhahn.

Sabel, Charles. 1982. *Work and Politics: The Division of Labor in Industry.* Cambridge: Cambridge University Press.

Sartori, Giovanni. 1970. "Concept Misformation in Comparative Politics." *American Political Science Review* 64, no. 4 (December): 1033–53.

———. 1976. *Parties and Party Systems.* Cambridge: Cambridge University Press.

Sauvigny, G. Bertier de. 1970. "Liberalism, Nationalism, Socialism: The Birth of Three Words," *Review of Politics* 32 (April).

Schieder, Wolfgang. 1979 [1974]. "Church and Revolution: Aspects of the Social History of the Trier Pilgrimage of 1844." Trans. Richard Deveson. In Clive Emsley, ed., *Conflict and Stability in Europe.* London: Croom Helm.

Schieder, Wolfgang, ed. 1983. *Liberalismus in der Gesellschaft des deutschen Vormärz.* Göttingen: Vandenhoeck und Ruprecht.

Schmitter, Philippe C. 1995a. "The Consolidation of Political Democracies: Processes, Rhythms, Sequences and Types." In Geoffrey Pridham, ed., *Transitions to Democracy: Comparative Perspectives From Southern Europe, Latin America and Eastern Europe.* Brookfield, VT: Dartmouth Publishing.

———. 1995b. "Transitology: The Sciences or the Art of Democratization?" In Joseph Tulchin with Bernice Romero, eds., *The Consolidation of Democracy in Latin America.* Boulder: Lynne Rienner.

Schmitter, Philippe C., and Terry Lynn Karl. 1993. "What Democracy Is . . . And Is Not." In Larry Diamond and Marc F. Plattner, eds., *The Global Resurgence of Democracy.* Baltimore: Johns Hopkins University Press.

Schneider, Ben Ross. 1995. "Democratic Consolidations: Some Broad Comparisons and Sweeping Arguments." *Latin American Research Review* 30, no. 2: 215–34.

Scully, Timothy. 1992. *Rethinking the Center: Party Politics in Nineteenth- and Twentieth-Century Chile.* Stanford: Stanford University Press.

Shamir, Michal. 1984. "Are Western Party Systems 'Frozen'? A Comparative Dynamic Analysis." *Comparative Political Studies* 17, no. 1 (April): 35–79.

Shanahan, William Oswald. 1954. *German Protestants Face the Social Question.* Notre Dame, IN: University of Notre Dame Press.

Sheehan, James J. 1971. "Liberalism and the City in Nineteenth-Century Germany." *Past and Present* 51:116–37.

———. 1978. *German Liberalism in the Nineteenth Century.* Chicago: University of Chicago Press.

Sikkink, Kathryn. 1991. *Ideas and Institutions: Developmentalism in Brazil and Argentina.* Ithaca: Cornell University Press.

Skocpol, Theda. 1979. *States and Social Revolutions: A Comparative Analysis of France, Russia and China.* Cambridge: Cambridge University Press.

Smith, Helmut Walser. 1995. *German Nationalism and Religious Conflict: Culture, Ideology, Politics, 1870–1914.* Princeton: Princeton University Press.

Smith, Michael Stephen. 1980. *Tariff Reform in France: The Politics of Economic Interest.* Ithaca: Cornell University Press.

Somers, Margaret R. 1993. "Citizenship and the Place of the Public Sphere: Law, Community, and Political Culture in the Transition to Democracy." *American Sociological Review* 58 (October): 587–620.

Sperber, Jonathan. 1984. *Popular Catholicism in Nineteenth-Century Germany.* Princeton: Princeton University Press.

———. 1991. *Rhineland Radicals: The Democratic Movement and the Revolution of 1848–1849.* Princeton: Princeton University Press.

———. 1995. "The Catholic Electorate in Imperial Germany." Paper presented at the American Historical Association Meetings, Chicago, January.

Stadelman, Rudolf. 1975 [1948]. *A Social and Political History of the German 1848 Revolution.* Trans. James G. Chastain. Athens: Ohio University Press.

Stearns, Peter N. 1974. *1848: The Revolutionary Tide in Europe.* New York: W. W. Norton.

Steinberg, Jonathan. 1976. *Why Switzerland?* Cambridge: Cambridge University Press.
Steinmo, Sven, and Kathleen Thelen. 1992. "Historical Institutionalism in Comparative Politics." In Sven Steinmo, Kathleen Thelen, and Frank Longstreth, eds., *Structuring Politics: Historical Institutionalism in Comparative Analysis.* Cambridge: Cambridge University Press.
Stengers, Jean. 1965. "Belgium." In Hans Rogger and Eugen Weber, eds. *The European Right.* Berkeley: University of California Press.
———. 1989. "Les consequences du suffrage universel tempéré, 1894–1919." In Hervé Hasquin and Adriaan Verhulst, eds., *Le Libéralisme en Belgique: Deux cents ans d'histoire.* Brussels: Centre Paul Hymans, Editions Delta.
Stephens, John D. 1979. "Religion and Politics in Three Northwest European Democracies." *Comparative Social Research* 2:129–57.
———. 1989. "Democratic Transition and Breakdown in Europe, 1870–1939: A Test of the Moore Thesis." *American Journal of Sociology* 94, no. 5 (March): 1019–77.
Strikwerda, Carl. 1997. *A House Divided: Catholics, Socialists, and Flemish Nationalists in Nineteenth Century Belgium.* Lanham, MD: Rowman and Littlefield.
Suval, Stanley. 1985. *Electoral Politics in Wilhelmine Germany.* Chapel Hill: University of North Carolina Press.
Tanner, Albert. 1988. "Bürgertum und Bürgerlichkeit in der Schweiz: Die 'Mittelklassen' and der Macht." In Jürgen Kocka, ed., *Bürgertum im 19. Jahrhundert: Deutschland im europäischen Vergleich.* Vol. 1. Munich: Deutscher Taschenbuch Verlag.
Tarrow, Sidney. 1994. *Power in Movement: Social Movements, Collective Action, and Politics.* Cambridge: Cambridge University Press.
Teuteberg, René. 1986. *Basler Geschichte.* Basel: Christoph Merian Verlag.
Thadden, Rudolf von. 1983. "Protestantismus und Liberalismus zur zeit des Hambacher Festes 1832." In Wolfgang Schieder, ed., *Liberalismus in der Gesellschaft des deutschen Vormärz.* Göttingen: Vandenhoeck und Ruprecht.
Therborn, Göran. 1977. "The Rule of Capital and the Rise of Democracy." *New Left Review*, no. 103 (May–June).
———. 1992. "The Right to Vote and the Four Routes To/Through Modernity." In Rolf Torstendahl, ed., *State Theory and State History.* London: Sage.
Thompson, J. M. 1967 [1955]. *Louis Napoleon and the Second Empire.* New York: W. W. Norton.
Thomson, David. 1969. *Democracy in France since 1870.* 5th ed. London: Oxford.
Tilly, Charles. 1988. "Misreading, Then Rereading Nineteenth-Century Social Change." In Barry Wellman and S. D. Berkowitz, eds., *Social Structures: A Network Approach.* Cambridge: Cambridge University Press.
Tocqueville, Alexis de. 1945 [1835/1840]. *Democracy in America.* 2 vols. Trans. Henry Reeve. New York: Vintage Books.
———. 1970. *Recollections.* Trans. George Lawrence. Ed. by J. P. Mayer and A. P. Kerr. New York: Doubleday.
Tolliday, Steven, and Jonathan Zeitlin. 1992. "Introduction: Between Fordism and Flexibility." In Steven Tolliday and Jonathan Zeitlin, eds., *Between Fordism and Flexibility.* Providence, RI: Berg.

Tudesq, André-Jean. 1964. *Les grands notables en France (1840–1849): Étude historique d'une psychologie sociale.* 2 vols. Paris: Presses Universitaires de France.

Ullrich, Hartmut. 1988. "Der italienische Liberalismus von der Nationalstaatsgründung bis zum Ersten Welkrieg." In Dieter Langewiesche, ed., *Liberalismus im 19. Jahrhundert.* Göttingen: Vandenhoeck and Ruprecht.

Valensise, Marina, ed. 1991. *François Guizot et la culture politique de son temps.* Paris: Editions du Seuil.

Valenzuela, J. Samuel. 1992. "Democratic Consolidation in Post-Transitional Settings: Notion, Process, and Facilitating Conditions." In Scott Mainwaring, Guillermo O'Donnell, and J. Samuel Valenzuela, eds., *Issues in Democratic Consolidation: The New South American Democracies in Comparative Perspective.* Notre Dame, IN: University of Notre Dame Press.

Vanhanen, Tatu. 1984. *The Emergence of Democracy: A Comparative Study of 119 States, 1850–1979.* Commentationes Scientarum Socialium 24. Helsinki: Finnish Society of Sciences and Letters.

Van Leynseele, Henry, and Jules Garsou. 1954. *Frère-Orban: Le Crépuscule, 1878–1896.* Brussels: La Renaissance du Livre.

———. 1997. *Prospects of Democracy: A Study of 172 Countries.* London: Routledge.

Verkade, Willem. 1965. *Democratic Parties in the Low Countries and Germany: Origins and Historical Developments.* Leiden: Universitaire Pers Leiden.

Vogel, Ursula. 1993. "Property Rights and the Status of Women in Germany and England." In Jürgen Kocka and Allan Mitchell, eds., *Bourgeois Society in Nineteenth-Century Europe.* Oxford: Berg.

Vorländer, Hans, ed. 1987. *Verfall oder Renaissance des Liberalismus?: Beiträge zum deutschen und internationalen Liberalismus.* Munich: Günter Olzog Verlag.

Weber, Eugen. 1976. *Peasants into Frenchmen: The Modernization of Rural France, 1870–1914.* Stanford: Stanford University Press.

———. 1980. "The Second Republic, Politics and the Peasant." *French Historical Studies* 11:521–50.

Weber, Max. 1978 [1921]. *Economy and Society: An Outline of Interpretive Sociology.* 2 vols. Berkeley: University of California Press.

Wehler, Hans Ulrich. 1985. *The German Empire, 1871–1918.* Trans. Kim Traynor. Leamington Spa and Dover, NH: Berg.

Weigel, George. 1990. "Catholicism and Democracy: The Other Twentieth-Century Revolution." In Brad Roberts, ed., *The New Democracies: Global Change and U.S. Policy.* Cambridge: MIT Press.

Weill, Georges. 1909. *Histoire du Catholicisme libérale in France, 1828–1908.* Paris: Félix Alcan.

———. 1928. *Histoire du parti républicain en France de 1814 à 1870.* Paris: Félix Alcan.

Welch, Cheryl. 1984. *Liberty and Utility: The French Ideologues and the Transformation of Liberalism.* New York: Columbia University Press.

White, Dan S. 1976. *The Splintered Party: National Liberalism in Hessen and the Reich, 1867–1918.* Cambridge, MA: Harvard University Press.

Whyte, John H. 1981. *Catholics in Western Democracies: A Study in Political Behaviour.* New York: St. Martin's.
Wilensky, Harold L. 1981. "Leftism, Catholicism, and Democratic Corporatism: The Role of Political Parties in Recent Welfare State Development." In Peter Flora and Arnold J. Heidenheimer, eds., *The Development of Welfare States in Europe and America.* New Brunswick: Transaction Books.
Williamson, John, ed. 1994. *The Political Economy of Policy Reform.* Washington, DC: Institute for International Economics.
Wintle, Michael. 1987. *Pillars of Piety: Religion in the Netherlands in the Nineteenth Century, 1813–1901.* Hull: Hull University Press.
Witte, Els, and Jan Craeybeckx. 1987. *La belgique politique de 1830 à nos jours: Les tensions d'une démocratie bourgeoise.* Translated from the Flemish by Serge Govaert. Brussels: Editions Labor.
Wright, Gordon. 1964. *Rural Revolution in France: The Peasantry in the Twentieth Century.* Stanford: Stanford University Press.
———. 1987 [1960]. *France in Modern Times: From the Enlightenment to the Present.* 4th ed. New York: W. W. Norton.
Zeldin, Theodore. 1963. *Émile Ollivier and the Liberal Empire of Napoleon III.* Oxford: Clarendon Press.
———. 1979a [1973]. *France, 1848–1945: Ambition and Love.* Oxford: Oxford University Press.
———. 1979b [1973]. *France, 1848–1945: Politics and Anger.* Oxford: Oxford University Press.
———. 1981 [1977]. *France, 1848–1945: Anxiety and Hypocrisy.* Oxford: Oxford University Press.
Zolberg, Aristide R. 1978. "Belgium." In Raymond Grew, ed., *Crises of Political Development in Europe and the United States.* Princeton: Princeton University Press.
———. 1986. "How Many Exceptionalisms?" In Ira Katznelson and Aristide R. Zolberg, eds., *Working-Class Formation: Nineteenth-Century Patterns in Western Europe and the United States.* Princeton: Princeton University Press.

Index

Agence générale pour la défense de la liberté religieuse, 51
Altenstein, Karl von, 69
Aminzade, Ronald, 54
Anderson, Margaret, 79
Anglican Church
  in Britain, 122
  in Ireland, 121–23
Anti-Catholicism
  of Protestant League in Germany, 83
  in Swiss Protestant cantons, 103
Anticlericalism
  in Catholic Europe, 32
  of Guizot's opponents, 53
Anticlericalism, Belgium
  as election issue (1912), 41–42
  of liberal movement, 25–26, 30–32, 35–36, 42
Anticlericalism, France
  historical roots in rural areas, 59
  in 1830 Revolution, 50, 54
  during Third Republic, 22, 56–63
Anticlericalism, Switzerland
  of Radical party, 108
Arblaster, Anthony, 9, 12

Barrot, Odilon, 4
Belgium
  cartel (1912), 41–42
  Catholic Church in, 31, 61
  Catholic party, 19, 34, 37, 39, 40–41, 119
  Catholic peasants, 119
  Constitution (1831), 27
  education system, 34–38, 40, 44
  elite and mass phases of liberal movement, 19

elite politics, 32, 43
franchise and suffrage in, 32–34, 40
independence (1830), 28
liberal and religious institutions, 40, 44
Liberal party, 32–40, 44, 119
mass base, 11
proportional representation, 40–41
Socialist party, 42
trade unions, 30, 32, 120
transition to democracy, 125
working class, 119–20
Biagini, Eugenio F., 8
Bigler, Robert M., 70
Blackbourn, David, 9, 14, 82, 83
Boulanger Affair (1889), France, 59
Breuilly, John, 9, 122

Calvinism, Switzerland, 92
Cantons, Swiss
  absence of liberal movements in assembly, 103
  anti-Catholicism in Protestant, 103
  churches in political structure of, 91–92
  conservative reaction to liberalism, 104–5
  conservatives in Luzern, 105
  conservatives in Zurich, 105
  under 1848 federal constitution, 107
  liberal constitutional regimes in, 94
  liberal movement in Valais, 101
  liberal movements in, 95–103
  liberal reform in Basel, 101–102
  liberal reform in Bern, 98–100
  liberal reform in Luzern, 100, 104
  liberal reform in Zurich, 95–98

152 Index

Cantons, Swiss (*continued*)
  opponents of liberalism in, 101
  political authority of Swiss, 90
  political power of urban elites in, 91
  role in Swiss Confederation, 88, 90
  secret pact (*Sonderbund*) of Catholic, 107
  structure of political systems in, 90–92
Cartel (1912), Belgium, 41–42
Catholic Center party, Germany
  under Kulturkampf policy, 81–83
  mobilization of Catholics by, 23
  support for (1870s and 1880s), 78–80
  as target of Protestant League, 83
  with universal suffrage, 79
Catholic Church
  Britain, 122
  drawing strength from liberal reforms, 44
  in Ireland, 121, 122
  "Josephine" view of, 100
  opposition to nineteenth-century liberalism, 127–28
  role in democratizing, 128
Catholic Church, Belgium
  autonomy granted by liberal reform, 21
  liberalism seen as opposition to, 31
  resistance to education law (1879), 61
Catholic Church, France
  opposition (1830s and 1840s), 54
  role in shaping republican dominance, 60–61
Catholic Church, Germany
  conservative movement in, 72–73
  effect of Kulturkampf policy on, 81–82
  under Falk Laws, 81
  implementation of political agenda, 85
  opposition to ultramontanism in, 74
  pilgrimages as demonstration of mobilization, 74
  See also Ultramontanism, Germany
Catholic Church, Switzerland
  under 1848 federal constitution, 107
  Jesuit Order banned (1848), 107
  liberal attacks on, 24, 106
Catholicism
  dominance in Belgium, 26–32
  Germany, 82
  Switzerland, 24
Catholic party, Belgium
  governments of (1884–1914), 19, 40
  introduction of proportional representation, 40–41
  liberal principles of, 119
  opposition to liberalism, 34
  reaction to plan for secular education, 19, 37, 39
  strength in rural areas, 37
Catholic party, Switzerland, 24
Catholics
  in Prussian parliament, 79
Chartier, Émile Auguste, 63
Churches
  in Swiss cantonal political structure, 91–92
Church of Scotland Act (1921), 123
Collier, David, 7
Collier, Ruth B., 7
Confederation, Swiss
  cantons in (1815), 88, 90
  political power of elites, 90
Conservatism, Germany, 70–71
Conservative party, United Kingdom, 123
Conservatives
  alliances with liberals in Germany, 23
  reaction to Swiss liberals, 104–5
Constitution (1815), Switzerland
  force of Restoration Constitution, 103
Constitution (1848), Switzerland
  federal authority of, 107
  limited male suffrage under, 108, 110
Constitutions
  of German states (1830s), 22
  Swiss cantonal, 94, 99
  Swiss federal (1848), 107–8, 110
  Swiss Restoration (1815), 103
Council of States, Switzerland, 107
Cousin, Victor, 53

Dahl, Robert, 124–25
Dahrendorf, Ralf, 8
D'Alviella, Goblet, 42
Democracies
  characteristics of nineteenth-century liberal regimes, 129–30
  liberal institutions as components of, 129
Democracy
  Belgian transition to, 25–26, 125
  effect of informal institutions in, 127
  French transition to, 45–48, 125–26, 127
  resistance in nineteenth-century, 126
  Swiss transition to, 125
  transition to and maintenance of, 12
de Ruggiero, Guido, 9, 13
De Schweinitz, Karl, 10
Diamond, Larry, 10, 127
Droz, Jacques, 70

Economic development
  as cause for regime change, 11–12
  effect on political institutions, 10
Education system, Belgium
  control of primary education by Catholic Church, 40
  effect of Church-secular struggle over, 36, 44
  liberals plan to secularize, 34–38, 44
  privileges of Catholic Church, 36
Education system, France
  opening of Catholic schools (1831), 51
  secularization of, 61–62
Eichorn, Johann, 70
Eley, Geoff, 9, 14
Elite phase
  Belgium, 25–32, 36, 43
  contribution to development of liberalism, 127–28
  definition of politics in, 18–19
  in France, 22, 45–48
  in Germany, 66–78
  as influence on European parties and regimes, 16–19
  in Switzerland, 23, 88, 90–103
Ellens, J. P., 8
Elwitt, Sanford, 13
Equality
  position of Belgian liberals on, 30
Evans, Richard J., 9, 14

Falk Laws (1873), Germany, 81
Federalist party, Switzerland, 104
Federal Societies, Swiss, 94
Fellenberg, Philipp von, 98–99
Fishman, Robert, 7
Flora, Peter, 11, 15
France
  anticlericalism, 50, 54, 56–63
  Catholic Church, 54, 60–61
  industrialization, 46–47
  liberalism in, 45–46, 49, 54
  mass base, 11
  opening of Catholic schools, 51
  Republican party, 45–46
  rise of working class, 13
  transition to democracy, 125–27
Franchise, Belgium
  attempts to broaden nineteenth-century, 33–34
  effect of narrow nineteenth-century, 32–33
  liberal formula to restrict, 34–35
Frère-Orban, Walther, 33
Friends of Light, Germany, 70–71, 76

German-Catholic movement
  liberalism of, 74–76
  minority of Catholics in, 77
Germany
  Catholic Center party, 78–79
  Catholic Church in, 72–74, 81–82, 85
  conservatism, 70–71
  Falk Laws (1873), 81
  Friends of Light, 70–71, 76
  German-Catholic movement, 74–78
  Kulturkampf policy, 81–84
  mass pilgrimage, 73–74, 77, 84
  Protestantism, 69, 72
  Protestant League, 83

Germany (*continued*)
  secularization, 82
  Social Democratic party, 80
  Socialist party, 78
  Ultramontanism, 72–73, 76–77
  unification under Prussian auspices (1870), 22
  universal suffrage, 79
Gerschenkron, Alexander, 10
Girard, Louis, 53
Gladstone, W. E., 122
Gregory XVI (pope), 51
Guizot, François, 52–53

Hall, John, 9
Haller, Carl L. von, 90
Hambacher Fest (1832), Germany, 69, 77
Haym, Rudolf, 69
Hengstenberg, Ernst Wilhelm, 69–70
Holden, Catherine, 75
Holmes, Stephen, 4
Huntington, Samuel, 128
Hymans, Paul, 42

Indemnity Bill (1866), Germany, 78
Industrialization
  Belgium, 25, 29
  in France during Third Republic, 46–47
  role of industrialists in Belgian politics, 29
  role of nineteenth-century, 10–11
Institutions
  autonomous religious and organizations, 129
  influence on liberal movements, 1
  informal patrimonialism and clientelism, 126
  liberal regimes ideas for new, 7–8
  in rational choice theory, 15–16
  related to marketization, 3
  role of liberal, 128–30
  structuring role of political, 14
Institutions, Belgium
  decline of liberal (1884–1914), 40
  role of religious, 44
Institutions, France
  interaction between liberalism and religious institutions, 49
  liberal institutions in, 62
Institutions, Germany
  secularization under Kulturkampf policy, 82
Institutions, religious
  influence in Belgium, 26–32
  influence on liberalism, 2
  interaction with political actors, 14
  in United Kingdom, 120
Interest groups
  politics of Protestant League in Germany, 83
  shaping political coalitions, 12–13

Janos, Andrew, 10
Janson, Paul, 33
Jardin, André, 13
Jenkins, T. A., 8
July Monarchy
  Orleanists in government of, 52
  pressure for parliamentary and electoral reform, 54
  religious issues in politics of, 53
  riots ending (1848), 54–55
  Thiers as supporter of, 56

Kalyvas, Stathis, 16, 61, 82
Kitschelt, Herbert, 10
Kocka, Jürgen, 9
Krieger, Leonard, 75–76
Kulturkampf policy, Germany
  effect of, 81–83
  failure of, 83
  as religious policy, 81
  repeal (1880s), 82–83
Kurth, James, 10
Küsnach Memorial, 97

Labour party, United Kingdom, 123
Lamennais, Hugues-Félicité-Robert de, 50–51

Lamennaisians
  Catholic Church reaction to politics of, 51
  politics of former, 51–52
Langewiesche, Dieter, 9
Lapolambara, Joseph, 6
Laski, Harold, 12
Law on Education (1879), Belgium, 35, 36
Lebovics, Herman, 13
Legitimists, France, 52
Leo XIII (pope), 81–82
Liberalism
  analysis of British, 8
  autonomous institutions critical for, 129
  based on socioeconomic development, 9–14
  connotations of nineteenth-century, 3
  core elements of, 3–5
  definition of, 2–5
  degrees of, 5
  as foundation for democratic political order, 129
  institutionalization shaping working-class activism, 123
  role of elites and masses in development of, 127–28
  in United Kingdom, 120
Liberalism, Belgian
  anticlericalism of, 30–31
  components of, 5
  dominance, division, and decline (1847–84), 32–38
  social basis, 32
Liberalism, British
  transition from elite to mass, 121
Liberalism, France
  ideas of Thiers, 4
  interaction with religious institutions, 49
  relationship between republicanism and, 54
  of Republican party, 45–46
  during Third Republic, 45
Liberalism, Germany
  support for, 22

  See also Kulturkampf policy, Germany
Liberalism, Switzerland
  in elite and mass periods, 23
  as political force (1848–1917), 23, 87
  See also Radical party, Switzerland
Liberalization
  defined, 129
Liberal movements
  emergence in nineteenth-century, 1, 6
  idea of national unity, 94–95
  strong and weak, 123
  successful, 128
  support from clergy, 1–2
Liberal movements, Belgium
  elite and mass phases, 19
Liberal movements, Britain
  influence of, 120
Liberal movements, Germany
  opposition to neoabsolutism, 23
  use of religion in, 66, 68
Liberal movements, Switzerland
  in cantons, 95
  oligarchies prior to reform, 24
  tenets and goals of (1815–31), 93–94
  working-class allies of, 109
Liberal parties
  characteristics of, 7
  explained through institutions and reform, 16–19
  political and religious institutions in development of, 15
Liberal party, Belgium
  anticlericalism of, 30–32
  defeat (1884), 37–44, 119
  development of liberal (1836, 1839), 29–30
  doctrinaire and progressive factions, 32–35
  under dominance of Catholic party, 40
  plan to secularize education, 34–38
  strength in urban areas, 37
  weakness in late nineteenth century, 39–40

156   Index

Liberal party, Switzerland
  supporters' shift to Radical camp, 109–10
Liberal party, United Kingdom
  base in nonconforming Protestant sects, 122
  Gladstone as leader of, 122–23
Liberal regimes
  Belgium, 19, 125
  explained through institutions and reform, 16–19
  factors influencing transitions to, 11–12
  forms of nineteenth-century, 7–8
  France, 21
  limited democracy in nineteenth-century, 125
  mass-based, 8
  political and religious institutions in development of, 15
  present-day democracies with characteristics of, 130
  Swiss transition to, 125
  transition in Europe to, 11–12, 125
Ligue de l'Enseignement, 56, 57–58
Lijphart, Arend, 25–26
Limongi, Fernando, 12
Lipset, Seymour, 10, 15, 48
Locke, Richard, 15
Longstreth, Frank, 15
Luebbert, Gregory M., 11, 14–15

Mace, Jean, 56
MacMahon, M. E. P. M., 57, 59
Madeley, John, 15
Malou, Jules, 37
Marian visions, Germany, 83
Marketization, 3
Marx, Karl, 13
Mass base
  Belgium, 11
  France, 11
Masses
  contribution to development of liberalism, 127–28
Mass phase
  Belgium, 32–43
  France, 22, 45–48, 56–63
  Germany, 77–83
  as influence on European parties and regimes, 16–19
  in Switzerland, 23–24, 103–9
Mass politics, 18–19
Mayeur, Jean-Marie, 60
Ménager, Bernard, 60
Michelet, Jules, 53
Middle class
  decline in interest in liberal reform, 13
  Germany, 23
  liberal mobilization in France, 22
  organized by Belgian Catholic party, 21
  politically active in Belgium, 25
  politics of, 12
  Switzerland, 24
Mill, John Stuart, 4
Mirari Vos, 51
Monarchy
  in Belgium prior to liberal reform, 19, 21
  in France prior to liberal reform, 22
  in Germany before liberal reform, 23
Monarchy, French constitutional (1830–48), 45–46, 48–56
  See also July Monarchy
Montalembert, Charles de, 51, 52, 53
Moses, Claire Goldberg, 52
Movements
  defined, 6
  of nineteenth century, 6
  See also Liberal movements
Müller, Thaddäus, 100
Munck, Gerardo, 129

National Council, Switzerland, 107
National unity, Swiss, 94–95
Neuenberg, Switzerland, 102
Nord, Philip, 129

O'Donnell, Guillermo, 126, 129
Oligarchies, Swiss, 24

Orleanists, France, 52
Ostrom, Elinor, 16

Parry, Jonathan, 8
Parties
   influences on European (1815–1914), 16–17
   nineteenth-century sense, 6
   See also Liberal parties; Political parties
Peasant, Trade and Citizens' party, 110–11
Peasants
   attempts in France to organize in agricultural syndicates, 59–60
   Germany, 23
   liberal mobilization in France, 22
   organized Catholic peasants in Belgium, 21, 32, 34, 36, 119
   republicanism and anticlericalism of French, 59–60
   Switzerland, 24
Pietism
   Germany, 71–72, 81
   Switzerland, 88, 104
Pilgrimages, German mass religiosity, 73–74, 77, 83
Pius IX (pope)
   antiliberalism of, 81
   ultramontanism under (1846–78), 73
Political organizations, Belgium
   founded in Church-secular education conflict, 36
Political parties
   Belgian liberal party as modern, 30
   definition of modern, 6–7
   founded by liberals, 23
Political systems
   churches in Swiss, 91–92
   effect of 1830 Revolution on, 50–51
   liberalization of, 12
   mass-based, 8
Politics
   in Belgium after 1884, 44
   elite phase, 16–19
   factors shaping, 14

   mass phase, 16–19
   of middle class, 12
   See also Mass politics
Presbyterian Church, Scotland, 121
Proportional representation
   Belgium, 40–41
   effect of 1919 switch in Switzerland to, 111–12
   Swiss Socialist party push for, 108
Protestant Church, Britain
   Anglican Church, 121
   dissenters from Anglican Church, 121–22
Protestantism, Germany
   anti-Catholicism of, 72
   conservatism, 70–71
   liberals drawing upon, 69
Protestantism, Switzerland, 24
   support for liberals, 105–6
Protestant League, Germany
   anti-Catholicism of, 83
Przeworski, Adam, 12

Quinet, Edgar, 53

Rabine, Leslie Wahl, 52
Radical party, Switzerland, 87, 104, 106–7
   alliance with Socialist party, 109
   anticlericalism of, 109
   formation of new party from within, 110–11
   as liberal party, 23
Rational choice theory, 15–16
Regimes
   defined, 7
   influences on European (1815–1914), 16–17
   See also Liberal regimes
Religion
   importance to French liberals, 54
   in liberal thought, 3–4
   role in elite and mass support for liberalism, 128
   use in German liberal movement, 66, 68

Religiosity, mass German, 73
Republicanism, France
  Masonic lodge of, 58
  as opposition under Second Empire, 56
  peasant, 59–60
  relationship between liberalism and, 54
  under Third Republic, 56–63
Republican party, France, 21, 45–46
Revolution (1830), France
  anticlericalism of, 50
  liberal thought of, 54
Rokkan, Stein, 15
Ronge, Johannes, 74
Rueschmeyer, Dietrich, 14, 48, 57, 65–66
Ruge, Arnold, 75
Ruggiero, Guido de, 13

Sabel, Charles, 14
Saint Simonianism, 51–52
Sartori, Giovanni, 7
Sauvigny, G. de Bertier de, 2
Schieder, Wolfgang, 73
Schmitter, Philippe, 129
Schneider, Ben Ross, 129
Schnell, Samuel, 99
Scully, Timothy, 15
Second Empire, France
  republican victory (1869), 57
Secularization
  of Catholic Center party in Germany, 82–83
  effect in Belgium, 34–38, 43–44
  under Kulturkampf policy in Germany, 82
Shanahan, William Oswald, 69–70
Sheehan, James J., 80
Shooting society, Swiss
  idea of national unity promoted by, 94
Siebenpfeiffer, Jacob, 69
Sintenis, F. W., 70, 71
Smith, Adam, 3
Smith, Helmut, 83
Snell, Ludwig, 96–97

Social classes. *See* Middle class; Working class
Social Democratic party, Switzerland, 109
Social Democratic party (SPD), Germany
  increasing support for (1880s and 1890s), 80
Socialist party, Belgium
  emergence, 42
  general strike (1913), 42
Socialist party, Germany
  growth of (1880s), 77
Socialist party, Switzerland
  alliance with Radical party, 109
  gains under proportional representation, 111
  push for proportional representation, 110
Societies, Swiss. *See* Shooting society, Swiss; Society for Natural Sciences, Swiss; Zofingen Society
Society for Natural Sciences, Swiss, 94
Sonderbund, 106–7
Sovereignty
  Belgian, 26
  of mass-based liberal systems, 8
  of monarchs in Germany, 23
Sperber, Jonathan, 82
State church, Prussian, 71–72
Steinmo, Sven, 15
Stephens, Evelyne, 14, 48, 57, 65–66
Stephens, John D., 14, 48, 57, 65–66
Suffrage, Belgium
  Catholic extension of broad, 40
  universal male (1893), 34, 40
Suffrage, Britain
  limited franchise in nineteenth century, 121
Suffrage, France
  election of 1876, 58–59
  first election with male (1848), 58
Suffrage, Germany
  effect of universal, 79
Suffrage, Switzerland
  limits in 1848 Constitution, 108, 110

Suffrage, United Kingdom
  universal (1919), 121
Suval, Stanley, 80
Switzerland
  anticlericalism, 108
  Calvinism, 92
  Catholic Church in, 106–7
  confederation, 88–90
  constitutions, 103, 107–8, 110
  liberalism in, 87
  liberal movements, 94–95, 109
  Pietism, 88, 104
  proportional representation, 111–12
  Radical party, 108–11
  shooting society, 94
  Social Democratic party, 109
  Socialist party, 109–11
  suffrage, 108, 110
  transition to democracy, 125
  workers' movement, 109
  working class, 109–10
  See also Cantons, Swiss

Tarrow, Sidney, 6
Test and Corporations Acts (1661, 1673), Britain, 121, 122
Thelen, Kathleen, 15
Thiers, Adolphe, 4, 53, 56, 57
Third Republic (1870–1940), France
  anticlericalism during, 56–63
  industrialization under, 46, 48
  liberalism during, 21, 45
Tilly, Charles, 6
Tocqueville, Alexis de, 54–55
Tolliday, Steven, 14
Trade unions, Belgium
  Catholic, 120
  Socialist, 120
Treaty of Twenty-Four Articles (1839), 29

Uhlich, Leberecht, 70–71

Ultramontanism, Germany
  achievements of, 73
  as conservative movement, 72–73
  as mass movement, 76–77
  opposition to liberal individualism, 73
Unionism, Belgium
  liberals drive to end, 30, 32
United Kingdom
  church-state relations, 121
  nineteenth-century liberalism, 120
  as parliamentary monarchy, 120

Vanhanen, Tatu, 131
Villmergen, Switzerland
  First War (1655–56), 92
  Second War (1712), 92
von Ebersol, Joseph Leu, 105, 106
von Struve, Gustav, 75

Weber, Eugen, 46
Wehler, Hans Ulrich, 13
Weigel, George, 128
Weiner, Myron, 6
Whyte, John H., 15
Wollstonecraft, Mary, 4
Workers' movement, Switzerland, 109
Working class
  as allies of Swiss liberal movement, 109–10
  Catholic and Socialist party loyalties in Belgium, 119–20
  demands for social justice, 13
  factors shaping activism of, 123
  organized for democracy, 130
  rise of French, 13
Wright, Gordon, 55

Zeitlin, Jonathan, 14
Zofingen Society, Switzerland, 94
Zolberg, Aristide, 13
Zwingli, Huldrych, 92